The Adventures of the COVID Hunter

Joseph Varon,
MD, FACP, FCCP, FCCM, FRSM

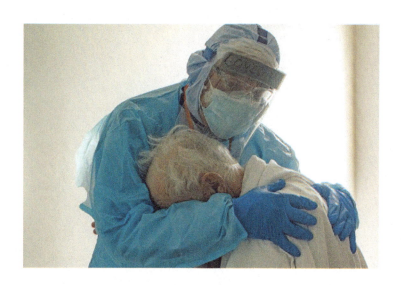

Dedication

This book is dedicated to:

- My late father, *Jacques Varon*, who taught me how to be a good human, and care for everyone regardless of gender, religion, or socioeconomic status.
- To my spouse, *Sara Varon*, for keeping up with me for 36 years and understanding that "patient care comes first".
- To my children (*Adylle, Jacques, Daryelle and Michelle*) and my Grandchildren (*Avi and Joseph*) for always being an inspiration for me to keep working.
- To all those patients who I could not save, and the millions that died during the pandemic. You taught me a big lesson and I will never forget.

Acknowledgement

I would like to express my deepest gratitude to Anita Elias for taking the time to review my book and providing valuable feedback. Her insightful comments and suggestions helped me to improve the overall quality of the book and refine its message.

Table of Contents

Prologue 1
The Reality of COVD-19 in the Hospital Setting 4
First Arrival to my Home 11
A Picture Says it All 13
The Milk Carton Thief 17
I Got Stuck on the Window 20
My Son is Running Naked on the Hallway 23
Divorce Court 25
The Heartwarming Letters 28
The Lonely Man 32
Death Threats 35
911: I Have Been Kidnapped 38
It is Too Hot in Here 42
Dueling Cardiac Arrests 45
I Miss My Wife on Thanksgiving 51
The Family that Bleeds Too Much 58
I Want a Donut 61
The Music Video 64
Can I Have Double Portions? 76
Let's Camp by the Window 79
The Escape Artist 82
The Man Who Did Not Believe in COVID-19 86
The Sex Worker 91
Massage My Back and I Will Give You 100 Dollars 95

The Man That Had Fun by Himself 100
The Conjugal Visit 104
The Screamer.. 107
The Birthday Party 111
About the Author... 118

Prologue

The COVID-19 pandemic changed the lives of billions of people around the World. Those of us in healthcare, had first contact with this "unknown" illness early in 2020 and over the past 3 years have seen a variety of unique situations affecting patients, families, clinics, hospitals, healthcare providers and governments. These day-to-day experiences have been unique in many instances and represent the most challenging times that I have witnessed in my life. Overall, the COVID-19 pandemic has brought about significant changes to almost every aspect of our lives.

The pandemic created a heightened sense of awareness around health and safety measures, including wearing masks, social distancing, and frequent hand washing. Many people shifted to remote work and online education. This resulted in changes to how people interact with colleagues and classmates, and how they balanced work and personal life. International and domestic travel were greatly impacted, with restrictions and quarantine measures in place in many countries. The pandemic had a significant impact on social interaction, with many people feeling isolated due to social distancing measures. Many social events were cancelled or postponed. Moreover, the pandemic caused the closure of many entertainment and leisure facilities, such as cinemas, theaters, and amusement parks. COVID-19 had a significant impact on the global economy, with many businesses closing down and people losing their jobs. In addition, a significant impact on mental health, with many people experiencing increased anxiety, stress, and depression due to the uncertainty and isolation caused by the pandemic.

But, what about healthcare professionals working in a COVID-19 unit? How did we cope with such changes? How did the patients cope with this unique situation?

This book depicts some of the interesting events, cases, and unique situations, that I witnessed in our COVID-19 unit during the pandemic. The names, ages and gender of the patients have been modified to ensure privacy. I have tried to include some of the patients that left me with a memory other than death and devastation. Some of the cases reflect human nature, the concern about the unknown issues in COVID-19, but most importantly, our quest for ending this devastating illness. I have not included in this book anything related to the long-term effects related to COVID-19, specifically the long-haul syndrome, as this is an evolving clinical entity at this time.

In many instances, when reading this book, you will be perplexed by some of the things we witnessed, and you will wonder how can that be possible? The fact is that COVID-19 brought the best and worst in people. The environment in a COVID-19 unit was terrifying for anyone coming into the ward. All doors closed, everyone wearing personal protective equipment (PPE), and in many instances double masks. I literally had to scream on regular basis for people to be able to hear what I was saying.

These cases represent chaos in a variety of ways. As a healthcare provider that have been working for several decades and confronted with massive catastrophes such as large earthquakes, with thousands of casualties, I felt that COVID-19 would not be as difficult. Yet, I was proven wrong. The number of critically ill patients entering our COVID-19 unit showed me that. No matter how prepared I thought our hospital was, no one was ready for this pandemic. The chaos in the COVID-19 units was universal.

Why *COVID HUNTER*? As many of you know, I have been featured in over 3400 television and radio interviews in the past 3 years, specifically discussing issues related to COVID-19. In the early days of the pandemic, I was a big proponent of making sure that people knew what was going on inside our units, as there were many people that did not believe in this devastating illness. Our hospital had a series of calls from different media outlets to allow them to visit our COVID-19 unit. It was the British Broadcasting Corporation (BBC), who on July 29, 2020, depicted me with the term "*COVID Hunter*" in their newscast. (https://www.bbc.com/news/av/world-us-canada-53576427).

Several colleagues had already used similar names for the work I was doing on this illness. Out of all the terms that were assigned to me "*COVID Hunter*" was the most precise, as it truly became my passion, to the point that even my license plates were personalized (CVD HTR). My late father (may he rest in peace), used to call me the "*COVID chaser*".

Joseph Varon, MD, FACP, FCCP, FCCM, FRSM

Houston, Texas

June 2023

The Reality of COVD-19 in the Hospital Setting

The COVID-19 pandemic had a significant impact on healthcare systems around the world, particularly in units that specialized in treating patients with the virus. These units, also known as COVID-19 wards, in most instances intensive care units (ICUs), were overwhelmed by the sheer number of patients requiring treatment, leading to overcrowding, shortages of essential medical supplies, and an increased risk of infection for healthcare workers.

In these units, patients with COVID-19 experienced severe respiratory distress, requiring the use of ventilators in many instances (particularly at the start of the pandemic) to assist with breathing. COVID-19 progressed rapidly in some patients, and some experienced complications such as blood clots, kidney failure, or pneumonia. Unfortunately, some patients who were admitted to COVID-19 units did not survive their illness, and healthcare workers were often faced with the difficult task of informing families of their loved ones' deaths.

Perhaps the most important part of the pandemic from my standpoint was the emotional toll of working in COVID-19 units, as healthcare workers witnessed multiple deaths in a single shift and were forced to make difficult decisions about prioritizing care when resources were limited. The desperation faced by patients, their families, and healthcare workers during the pandemic was compounded by the fear and uncertainty surrounding the virus. Patients were isolated from their loved ones, and families were unable to visit their relatives in the hospital due to infection control measures. Healthcare workers faced shortages of personal protective equipment (PPE) and other essential supplies, increasing their risk of infection, and making it more difficult to provide care.

Overall, the reality of COVID-19 units was one of high stress, exhaustion, and loss, as healthcare workers struggled to keep up with the demands of caring for patients during a global pandemic.

For those of you who do not know me, I am a doctor that has multiple specialties, but my true passion is the care of those who are acute and critically ill. I have been doing this for decades and I became a "COVIDOLOGIST" at the start of the pandemic. As a critical care medicine professional, I had training in basic epidemiology, diagnostic testing techniques and the management of complications in deadly ill patients. However, COVID-19 was completely different. What I knew is that I was not ready and the hospital that I worked at was not either. I had to establish a plan of action before these cases started to show up in our city.

First, I needed to know how many people would be positive for COVID in the Houston metropolitan area. That was a very difficult task. With the aid of the Chief Operating Officer at our hospital, we launched a COVID-19 drive-through testing campaign that to date (in a period of 5 weeks) had tested more than 22,000 individuals with an 8.6% positive percentage of individuals. We had 5 different testing sites that worked very efficiently. Clearly, this was a small number of tests compared to the population of the 4th largest city in the United States. By the time this book was written, or institution had tested more than 1.2 million individuals for COVID-19.

Second, I had to allocate an area that would be exclusive for caring for these patients within the confines of the hospital grounds. We initially closed 2 wards in our hospital and converted them into state-of-the art negative pressure wards. That is a system that would, literally isolate such areas from the rest of the hospital. We added every element to assure complete decontamination and made sure that everyone that worked in this unit was properly trained in such containment techniques. A comprehensive list of protective equipment was created and obtained. Rigorous check lists for everyone working in the COVID-19 unit were utilized to assure compliance.

Third, and probably the most difficult task, was to find personnel willing to work with these patients. By far, this was the most difficult task of caring for a patient with COVID-19. Not only many healthcare providers refused to care for the COVID-19 positive patients, but this reminded me of the first few patients that I saw as a medical student in the 1980s with the human immunodeficiency virus (HIV) and subsequent acquitted immunodeficiency syndrome (AIDS). At that time, no one wanted to care for them as they were afraid of "catching" the disease.

Fourth, I needed to have a COVID-19 specialty clinic to follow those patients that survived their hospitalization or those positive patients that needed a clinician to see them. We added a wing to the hospital that would be used only for patients that tested positive and that needed follow up. In such area, a state-of-the-art imaging department allocated exclusively for these patients and a dedicated team of healthcare providers to follow them.

As you can see, this was our reality in the COVID-19 unit. Forget about everything you heard or saw on television or radio. COVID-19 truly turned hospitals into chaos. Every single medical institution suffered through this pandemic. Most were not prepared for a healthcare emergency of this magnitude and many of us had to improvise.

When I first had to create our COVID-19 unit, I reviewed some of the approaches that had been taken in those countries that had a head start on this illness, such as China. It was clear, that this was a highly contagious disease with a high mortality rate. At that time, the mode of transmission was still a bit of a mystery and we had to protect ourselves.

It is very difficult to comprehend the emotional state that healthcare providers would have when confronted with critically ill COVID-19 patients. On the one hand, we wanted to save the patient's life, while on the other, we were scared that in the process, we would lose our own life. In our own institution, our COVID-19 unit had only 3 doctors that would come in to see patients, as everyone else was scared. I, literally lived in the unit and worked non-stop for 715 continuous days. Some days I would work up to 20 hours to get to my home and try to sleep for a few hours, with multiple phone calls in between.

As this illness was a shock to all the healthcare providers, many of the interventions that were being tried had unexpected consequences. In our institution, we elected to use medications that were fully approved by the Food and Drug administration for treatment and in some instances, we used research protocols that we developed and were approved by an independent Institutional Review Board to assure that the safety and privacy of the patients were completely considered. Many would consider that many of the treatments in the COVID-19 units were trial-and-error. I remember that early in the pandemic, the then Governor of New York kept on asking funding for "ventilators" (respirators), with the misconception that patients needed to be placed on these life-support devices to save them from death. Yet, just a few months later, we found that such intervention was a terrible idea and that we had to do everything in our power to prevent patients from being on one of those machines, as the mortality rate of patients that have been placed on them exceeded 88 percent. Yes, we changed our point of view regarding interventions repeatedly.

What was even worse is that throughout the country, there was no homogenous message as to how to deal with a COVID-19 patient. The President of the United States would say something, the head of the National Institutes of Health something completely opposite (and then change his mind several times), the head of the Centers for Disease Control something different, the head of the

World Health Organization something else and some of the key opinion leaders, including myself, would provide a different strategy. Those who followed the news, could not identify who to follow. As a practicing healthcare provider, this made my life even more difficult. We had no true guidance. COVID-19 had become a political illness. An illness that was killing patients, mostly because there was no consensus of what to do for them. Indeed, many of my professional colleagues used therapeutic interventions that made no scientific sense and advocated for such treatments.

An area that is extremely important to mention in this book, is how we felt inside the COVID-19 units. The emotional toll of working in a COVID-19 unit cannot be overstated. Healthcare workers all over the World were often working under highly stressful conditions, dealing with the physical and emotional needs of their patients while also managing their own fears and anxieties about contracting the virus. The high number of deaths in COVID-19 units every single day were emotionally overwhelming, and many healthcare workers struggled with feelings of grief and loss. You cannot imagine the number of nurses that would approach me every day, while in the middle of my rounds, crying because we had lost one or more patients that day. Additionally, the isolation and separation that occurs in COVID-19 units made it very difficult for healthcare workers to debrief or receive support from their colleagues.

So how did I cope with all this tragedy? I have always had a sense of humor, and I made sure that my staff would use techniques aimed at working as a team. I decorated our COVID-19 unit with unit images and decided to keep a daily "counter" of how many days had we worked non-stop. Each day, the nurses and other healthcare providers would print the iconic numbers that I had on the wall with different themes, depending on the time of the year. Another technique was to decorate our PPE, which made us unique. I also requested that every single healthcare provider in full PPE should have a picture of themselves hanging from the neck, as patients were afraid of not knowing who was caring for them. Most patients would enjoy getting a better idea of who was caring for them with these images. Of course, at times, we would all use cartoons to make our days better. It was chaos! And laughter was a good way to cope with stress.

Each of the cases and situations depicted in this book show real situations that I saw over the pandemic, and the struggles that sometimes we had. Many of us maybe too quick to criticize the response time, and situations depicted, but make no mistake, these COVID-19 units were chaotic. We all did our very best to aid our patients.

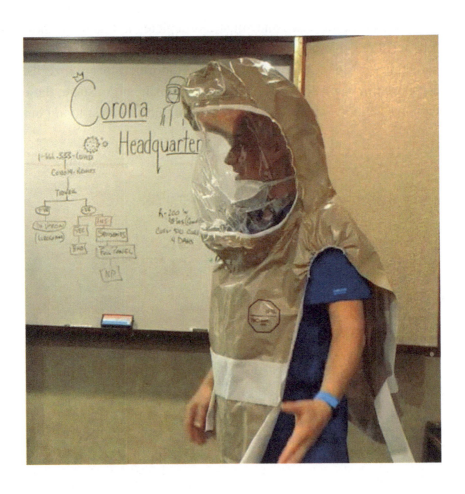

First Arrival to my Home

After a couple of days of working non-stop in our COVID-19 unit, I went home to eat and get some sleep. I remember vividly opening the gate and parking my car. As our home was lifted during one of the Houston floods, I saw Sara, my spouse, signaling me to get out of the car. Once I was out of my vehicle, from the floor above me, she screamed *"please take off all your clothes"*. You can imagine my smile at that point! I thought "wow, she wants me naked.... this has not happened in many years". I promptly complied with the unusual request. As I was starting to think about what her next move would be, suddenly she threw me a large black trash bag from where she was to the floor and told me *"Now, place all your clothes and shoes inside the trash bag"*. Again, I complied with the instructions, but this time my hopes of some romantic encounter were fading away.

As soon as I placed all the items on the trash bag, Sara again gave additional instructions *"Take the trash bag to the laundry room and place all the items in the washer, then go upstairs, take a shower and then you can come and say hi!"*.

I cannot imagine the anxiety that she had thinking that I would bring a deadly disease into the household and the implications that this had. It was so early in the pandemic, that we truly did not know what was going on with the illness. I know multiple medical colleagues that moved out of their homes in the first 6 months of the pandemic and either lived in the hospital or rented a hotel room. I can tell you that healthcare workers who worked in COVID-19 units during the pandemic faced immense challenges and stresses. They were often working long hours, with limited resources and facing the risk of infection. Many have had to isolate themselves from their families and loved ones to reduce the risk of transmission. Many of them died. Yet, despite these challenges, healthcare workers showed incredible resilience, dedication, and commitment to their patients and the communities they serve. While coming home from work in a COVID-19 unit may not necessarily be characterized by excitement, healthcare workers who worked tirelessly during the pandemic deserve my gratitude and appreciation for their bravery and selflessness in the face of such adversity.

A Picture Says it All

The first few days in my COVID-19 unit were very hard. The patients all feared the unit. The primary reason was that they did not know who was caring for them. At the time, I was the chief of staff at our hospital and director of the COVID-19 unit and needed to find a way to provide hope and comfort for the patients. As the virus swept across the world, healthcare workers faced unprecedented challenges, including the difficulty of connecting with patients who were isolated and unable to see the faces of their caregivers. At that point, I found a way to bridge the gap and provide a sense of connection for the patients by wearing a laminated photo of each healthcare provider outside their PPE. It was a small, yet powerful gesture that quickly caught on among our colleagues and became a symbol of their commitment to providing care and comfort in a time of crisis.

My decision to wear a photo of myself outside my PPE was born out of a desire to connect with my patients on a personal level. As I explained in an interview with CNN, "*When I talk to them, I say, 'You know, I'm not only your doctor, I'm your friend.' And it's not only me. It's everybody who's taking care of you. We're all your friends. We're all here to help you.*" For many patients, being cared for by someone whose face they couldn't see was a source of anxiety and fear. By wearing a photo of the healthcare provider, we were able to provide a visual representation of who we were and establish a rapport with these frightened patients.

Every single healthcare provider that would enter the COVID-19 unit at our hospital would get their picture taken, laminated, and placed around their neck. We followed strict cleaning protocols, so that the pictures would be sanitized every time we left the patient's rooms. However, sanitizing laminated photos is not as simple as wiping them down with a disinfectant wipe. The lamination can make it difficult for the disinfectant to penetrate and effectively kill the virus. We tried a variety of ways to do this without damaging the pictures. One option was to use a UV-C light sanitizing device. These devices use ultraviolet light to kill bacteria and viruses, including the novel coronavirus. We placed the laminated photos in the device for a few minutes to sanitize them. We also used a hydrogen peroxide vapor system. These systems use a fine mist of hydrogen peroxide to disinfect surfaces and equipment. A third option that we utilized was a simple solution of bleach and water. Regardless of the method used, we always followed the manufacturer's instructions for cleaning and sanitizing.

Sanitizing laminated photos may seem like a small detail, but for healthcare workers who wore them, it made a big difference. These photos served as a reminder to patients that they were being cared for by real people who were dedicated to their wellbeing. By taking the time to sanitize these photos, healthcare workers were not only protecting themselves and their patients from the virus, but also preserving a symbol of hope and connection in a time of crisis.

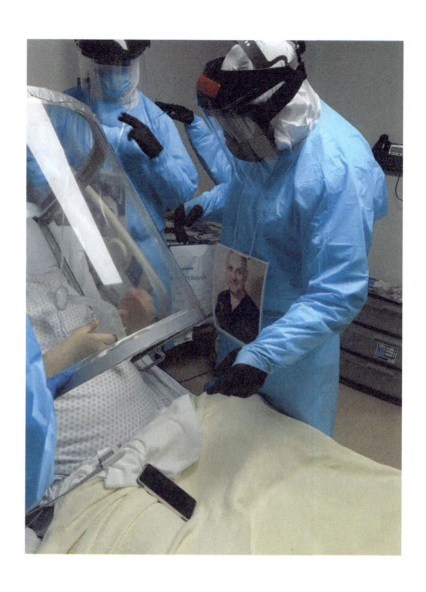

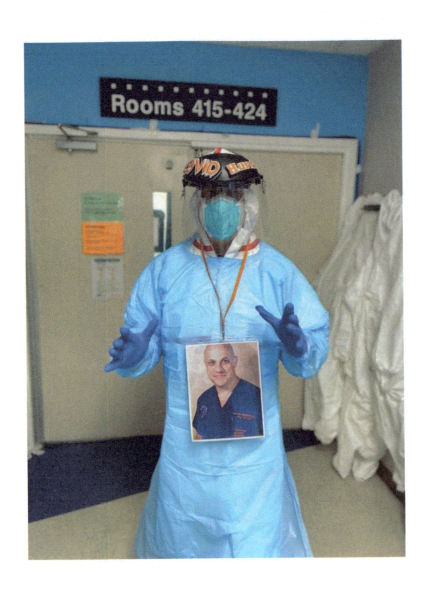

The Milk Carton Thief

A 38-year-old gentleman was admitted to our COVID-19 unit with complaints of fever, shortness of breath and found to have low oxygen levels. He had no other medical history, did not smoke, and did not use any drugs. On arrival to the unit, he was awake, alert, oriented, requiring supplemental oxygen via a nasal cannula. His blood pressure was low, requiring the administration of intravenous fluids. When assessed by the nurse, he indicated that he was hungry, so a food tray containing a sandwich, fruit and orange juice was promptly provided to him.

Within 24 hours of hospital admission, his vital signs stabilized, and he was able to start walking (with oxygen). That same night, when he received his dinner, he requested a small carton of milk. Such request was immediately addressed. Within minutes of finishing his milk carton, the patient pressed the emergency call button by his bed and as soon as the healthcare providers arrived at his room and asked him what was going on, he indicated that he needed "a second milk carton as soon as possible". The nurse caring for the patient asked him as to the reason for such request. He indicated that he loved milk.

That same night, the patient removed his oxygen and started to walk in the hospital hallways and began entering the rooms of the other patients. As he approached each room, he went directly to their food trays looking for milk. This was all documented in the video-security system that the COVID-19 rooms had. As soon as the nursing staff recognized what was going on, the suited up on personal protective equipment and went looking for this man. Once the caught him, he had 6 additional cartons of milk with him that he was juggling to transport back to his room.

The next morning while reviewing the images from the prior night and doing my rounds, I confronted the patient regarding this illicit activity, and the issues related to patient privacy. On my examination he was fully awake, alert and had no signs of any mental derangement. When asked about his unusual behavior, the patient stated, "*I just like milk*".

The night prior to his hospital discharge, the patient decided to take another stroll on the hallway, and this time from the distance assess who had milk by their bedside. As soon as he was going to enter the room of another patient, one of the nurses ran to stop him and returned with him to his room. Hours later, and in good clinical condition the patient was discharged to follow up in our outpatient clinic, where he never showed up after discharge.

I am sure you are wondering, why would someone steal milk cartons? Why would someone go into someone else's room and do such a thing? It is difficult to speculate about the motivations behind why someone would steal milk cartons from other patients, especially in the context of a COVID-19 unit. The fact is that the COVID-19 units got us to recognize behaviors that many of us have not seen in decades of practicing medicine.

From a medical standpoint, patients may have cravings for unique types of food. We call this "pica", and it is usually associated to specific nutritional deficiencies (such as iron, calcium, etc.). However, in this patient, I found no evidence of any form of nutritional deficiency.

In these situations where nurses observed patients doing something illegal in the COVID unit, such as stealing milk, they experienced a range of emotions, such as shock, concern, and fear for the safety of themselves and their colleagues, as stealing may indicate violent behavior. Nurses are trained to handle difficult situations and follow proper protocols when dealing with any issues that arise in a medical setting. However, situations such as this one, are unique. The nurses in our COVID-19 unit during the pandemic commonly felt frustrated or angry that patients were not following rules or guidelines, which could endanger the health and safety of themselves and others in the unit.

I Got Stuck on the Window

A 57-year-old morbidly obese lady was admitted to our unit with a 2-week history of shortness of breath, cough, and fever. In the emergency department she was found to have a significant low oxygen level, a positive COVID-19 test and radiographic findings compatible with COVID-19 pneumonia. She was awake, alert, and coherent and could tell us the reasons why she ended up in the hospital. She had a history of high blood pressure and diabetes that had poor medical control.

Standard management of such patients included the use of potent steroids, to reduce the inflammation in the lungs, in hope to improve the oxygenation. We used our "cocktail" of medications on this lady and her symptoms and oxygenation improved remarkably after 72 hours of hospital admission.

The patient had been talking daily over the phone with her family, as there were no visitors allowed in the hospital because of an order of the County Judge in our area. As the hospital was a single-story building, some families would "park" outside the patient's windows and talk to them over the phone.

By the fourth day of hospitalization the patient complained to the nurses that she was very anxious as she could not see the faces of the healthcare providers (as we all were using personal protective equipment). Her anxiety was such that in a couple of instances she pulled all the wires that were attached to her vital signs monitor and tried to get out of her room into the hallway of the COVI-19 unit. Fortunately, the video camera system installed on the hallway recognized such activity and the nurses went immediately to her room and "calmed her down" and placed her back on her bed.

At 5 o'clock in the morning, on day 5 of hospitalization, I received a frantic phone call from the nurse caring for this patient. Apparently, she had removed all her clothes and wires that connected her to the monitors and went straight to the window. She opened it and tried to get out by sliding her body through the window. As she was morbidly obese, after her head and arms made it thought the window, the rest of the body "got stuck". The nurse realized this was going on and tried to gently pull her back, but she remained stuck. On my arrival to her room, multiple healthcare providers and security officers were trying to get the patient into the room, but she was truly stuck. The options we had were limited. As it was a cold morning of January, I was truly concerned she would develop hypothermia while we were trying to remove her from the window. Along with security, we elected to "push from the outside" while extending her arms, while the nurses on the inside pulled gently. I was quite concerned, as all patients in our COVID-19 unit were receiving blood thinners and she could have a significant bleed if we didn't do this correctly.

After several failed attempts, one last try resulted in successful dislodging from the window. Amazingly, she had no injuries related to this. The patient was placed back in her bed and reattached to all the monitoring systems. Surprisingly her vital signs remained stable and did not have any evidence of hypothermia. A 24-hour-a day sitter was assigned to her bed, so that this would not happen again.

Over the next 72 hours, the patient's condition improved, her mental status got better and was able to be discharged in good condition to the care of her family. On follow up at our outpatient clinic she was very apologetic for the incident, indicating that she had no recollection of what had transpired.

This case taught me several lessons. First, if a patient gets stuck on a window while trying to escape from a hospital during the COVID-19 pandemic, the first priority is to ensure the patient's safety and well-being. Next, alert security personnel and other staff members to come and help the patient while coordinating with the hospital's emergency response team to ensure a prompt and effective response. Sometimes it may be necessary to call for specialized rescue services such as a fire department or search and rescue team. As patients may be scared or disoriented while attempting to escape, especially during the COVID-19 pandemic, it is essential to provide them with comfort and reassurance while they are stuck. If the patient is attempting to escape due to fear of contracting COVID-19, healthcare providers should ensure that appropriate protocols are being followed to minimize the risk of infection. But the most important lessons is that healthcare providers should try to understand the patient's motivation for attempting to escape. If the patient is experiencing anxiety, fear, or other emotional distress, it may be necessary to provide them with additional support or counseling services.

My Son is Running Naked on the Hallway

While working on our COVID-19 unit it was not uncommon to have several members of the same family with various degrees of illness. In some instances, we had several of them on assisted ventilation (life-support) simultaneously. On this occasion, we were caring for 3 members of the same family. The mother, a 69-year-old lady with history of diabetes that had fallen ill 10 days prior to admission and that required hospitalization due to low levels of oxygen. Her husband, a 72-year-old man who had cardiac (heart) complications of COVID-19, and their son, a previously healthy 32-year-old-man who had severe covid requiring high amounts of supplemental oxygen and intensive care. This young man was being treated with high doses of steroids (cortisone-like agents) to decrease the amount of inflammation in his lungs, in addition to our standard COVID-19 protocol.

After 72 hours of being in the hospital, one night, the 69-year-old lady pressed the emergency button in her bed several times. When the nurses called backed to check on her, she told them *"my son is running naked on the hallway"*. The nurses immediately accessed the hallway cameras and realized that, indeed, the young man was totally naked running on the hallway trying to leave the COVID-19 unit. Apparently, the door on the mother's room was open and she glanced at the "runner" and recognized him as her own son. The nurses promptly gowned-up and got inside the unit where they were able to reach the patient and smoothly brought him back to his room. Upon examination, he was confused, somewhat combative, and had oxygen levels below normal. He was placed on oxygen immediately and reconnected to the monitor. A 24-hour a day sitter was kept at his bedside to prevent this from happening again. Further evaluation revealed no injuries. A detailed neurological examination, including brain imaging was totally unrevealing. The primary assumption was that the high doses of steroids had been the culprits of his behavior. Days later, his mentation had returned to normal. Of interest, this young man had never had any psychiatric issues nor used drugs of abuse.

COVID-19 patient's behavior during the pandemic, could be affected by a variety of factors, including mental health issues, substance abuse, medication side effects, and stress or anxiety related to being in a medical setting or experiencing a serious illness. It was also possible that our patients may have been disoriented or confused due to their illness or medication, leading to the unusual behavior of running naked on the hallway.

Divorce Court

Early in the pandemic, the overwhelming number of cases we got admitted to the hospital required that many of the rooms would have two bed to accommodate 2 patients at a time. On several occasions, when we had couples that needed admission at the same time, we made every effort to accommodate them in the same room, so they would keep company to each other. You must understand that these isolation rooms were quite gloomy, as the doors were always closed, and no visitation was allowed per order of the County judge.

On this occasion, we admitted a couple. He was a 56-year-old gentleman without any major medical history that fell ill to COVID-19 a week prior to admission. He had significant respiratory issues and low oxygen that required intensive monitoring and treatment in our unit. His wife of 23 years was a 49-year-old lady with history of diabetes mellitus and obesity that had similar symptoms with lower oxygen levels than her husband.

The night that this couple was admitted was particularly busy. We had several patients experiencing cardiac arrests and resuscitation efforts were non-stop. When the night nurse came to check on both patients at 1 a.m., they were both sleeping and has good vital signs. The monitor did not show any evidence of decompensation for the next several hours.

The next morning, when I came to see the patients, I was warned by the morning nurse, that they were very upset and wanted to talk to me immediately regarding their hospital accommodations. As this was a common occurrence during COVID-19, I expected them to complain about the lack of visitors in their room, or the fact that we all had to go in full PPE to see them. I was totally wrong!

As soon as I entered the room, the husband looked at me and said, "*get me out of this room immediately*". He was clearly upset and before I inquired why was he so upset with the room, his wife screamed "*make sure he goes to another hospital and is far away from here*". I was still confused at the time, as I could not imagine what was so bad, that even the spouse wanted him to be away.

As soon as they both allowed me to speak, I asked them "why"? The wife looked at me and said, "*isn't it obvious*"? "*He is an absolute idiot, and I do not want to be on the same room as he*". The husband followed that by "*this is what I deal with every day, get me out of here*". This was followed by a series of interactions that included many insults by both patients against each other.

As this was clearly a significant issue and concerned that all the screaming and fighting could cause more damage to these patients' oxygenation, I immediately requested the assistance of the charge nurse to find another room to allocate one of the 2 disrupting patients. We were able to move the husband to the other end of the ward where he remained for the rest of his hospital stay.

During their stay both patients had a good clinical recovery. As I got to know them better, I found out that they had been arguing for quite a long period of time and had considered divorce. As noted in some of the other cases, COVID-19 brought out the best and worst in many individuals and it was not uncommon to see these situations. Indeed, the fact that everyone was under lockdown for a period of time, increased the number of divorces throughout the World.

The husband left the hospital 2 days after his wife to be followed by their primary care provider. On a phone call after discharge, they both indicated that they were living together and that they were trying to resolve some issues they had.

It is important to realize that the COVID-19 pandemic had a significant impact on many aspects of life, including divorce. The pandemic caused significant stress and anxiety for many people, particularly those who have lost jobs or loved ones due to the virus. This placed a strain on relationships and increased the likelihood of divorce. To make things worse, in some areas, the court systems were overwhelmed with COVID-related cases and had to delay or reschedule divorce proceedings. This prolonged the divorce process and increase stress for those involved. COVID-19 also caused significant economic hardship for many people, which was, in many cases, a contributing factor in divorce. Couples were struggling to pay bills, manage debt, or provide for their families, which placed a strain on their relationship.

Overall, while the pandemic has certainly created unique challenges for those going through a divorce, it is important to remember that every situation is different. Our patients had significant issues and being deadly ill made things worse, yet they tried to work things out.

The Heartwarming Letters

During the pandemic, not everything was bad. I remember how in late October 2020, when I sat at my desk in his small office, I was surrounded by stacks of letters and envelopes. The room was filled with an air of gratitude and appreciation. It had been months since the COVID-19 pandemic had taken over the world, and I only thought about hope and stayed resilient. As the head of the COVID-19 unit at United Memorial Medical Center (UMMC), I had tirelessly fought against the virus, working hundreds of days without rest.

To be honest, I was surprised that my dedication had not gone unnoticed. Among the stacks of letters were hundreds of heartfelt messages from people all over the world who had seen our work on various news outlets. These letters were expressions of gratitude, admiration, and encouragement. Each one held a unique story, a personal account of how our efforts had touched their lives. I would read every letter I received. For example, one was from a young woman in Spain whose mother had been battling COVID-19 in the hospital. She wrote about the fear and uncertainty that had gripped her family during those dark days. But it was one of the news interviews that I had done that had brought them hope. She thanked me for my tireless efforts and for being a beacon of light in the midst of the storm.

I read each letter, one by one. There were stories of recovery, of lives saved, and of loved ones lost. But in every single letter, there was an overwhelming sense of gratitude and admiration for our unwavering commitment. People from all walks of life, from different corners of the globe, had taken the time to express their thanks to us. Their words were a powerful reminder of the impact we were making, even in the face of unimaginable challenges.

One particular letter caught my attention. It was from a fellow doctor in South Africa who had been inspired by our work. He wrote about the long hours he had spent in the COVID-19 unit at his own hospital and how he often felt exhausted and defeated. But hearing about our work and resilience had given him renewed strength and determination. The South African doctor thanked me for being a role model and for showing him what it truly meant to be a healthcare hero.

These letters served me as a reminder of the global impact of the pandemic and the collective struggle to overcome it. They were a testament to the human spirit, to the resilience and strength that emerged during times of crisis. But above all, they were a testament to the power of compassion and the profound difference that we could make.

I thought about the countless sleepless nights, the sacrifices we made, and the toll it had taken physically and emotionally. But in that moment, as I read those letters, it all seemed worth it. It wasn't about personal recognition or accolades; it was about knowing that our work had touched lives and brought comfort to those in need.

I also realized that I was not alone in this fight. The letters became a source of strength and inspiration, reminding me that I was part of a global community of healthcare workers who were all working tirelessly to combat the virus. The words of gratitude fueled my determination to continue the battle against COVID-19, no matter how difficult the road ahead might be.

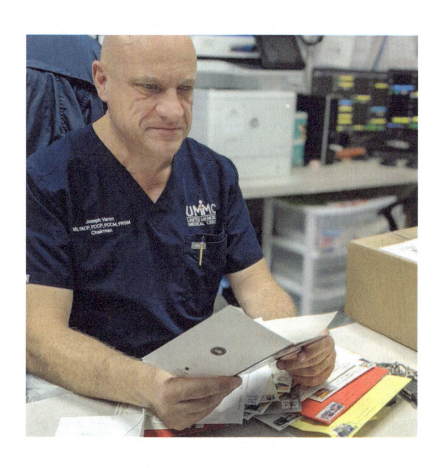

The Lonely Man

On the morning of Christmas day 2020, we admitted a 48-year-old man to our COVID-19 unit with complaints of shortness of breath, fever, and cough of one week duration. This gentleman had no significant prior medical history and was taking no daily medications. His oxygenation levels were very low, and his radiographic images were quite concerning. He had been admitted to a single-bed room, which at that time were quite uncommon, as we had 2 patients in most rooms due to the severity of the situation. The nurse caring for him, asked him about any family members, and he declined to answer such question.

On hospital day 2, he was somewhat better with the treatment that we were providing. His oxygen levels were improving, and he was less short of breath. We found out that he had been homeless for several months and that he had no close relatives in the area.

On that same night, I remember receiving a call from our nurses indicating that the patient was no longer in his room. Security was looking for him outside the hospital, assuming he had "escaped" the unit, like many of the other patients have tried to do in the past. Review of the security cameras depicted him leaving his room and going through the hallways. At some point, in an area of a blind spot, we could not assess where he was. At that point, my staff went and physically checked every room in the unit in case he had gotten confused and ended up in another room. To our surprise, we found him in the same bed as another patient, who was on a mechanical ventilator and comatose. The nurses immediately removed him from such room and took him to his room, where he was reattached to his monitor and kept with a sitter at his bedside. I came to see him personally at that time to make sure he was fine and that the other patient had not had any issues related to this man sleeping on his bed. When I asked the patient, why did he go to the other man's bed, he indicated that *"he was feeling lonely"*. We spoke about how unusual this situation and he was feeling scared, as he had been able to learn that COVID-19 was deadly, and he did not want to be alone. Over the next few days his condition improved dramatically, and we were able to make arrangements for him to be able to go to a shelter upon discharge.

For a second, place yourself in his shoes. This poor man, had no family, was homeless and now had an illness that appeared to be lethal in many instances. The motivation for this patient to be close to others was not totally unheard off. The fact that he could not even see the healthcare providers' faces as we were fully protected with our equipment and masks, made it very difficult to accept what was going on and some looked for company. In that sense, we always tried to pair people in rooms with similar backgrounds and language, in an attempt to minimize loneliness.

Being a lonely man in a COVID-19 unit was an incredibly difficult and isolating experience not only for this patient, but for many people around the World. Patients with COVID-19 were often isolated from others to prevent the spread of the virus, which means that they were unable to see their family and friends in person during their hospitalization. For men who were already dealing with feelings of loneliness or social isolation, such as our patient, being in a COVID-19 unit could only exacerbate those feelings. The lack of social interaction and support from others lead in many patients to feelings of depression, anxiety, and hopelessness. In addition, patients in COVID-19 units were dealing with physical symptoms such as shortness of breath or chest pain, which were in many instances frightening and further contributed to feelings of isolation and fear.

Healthcare workers in COVID-19 units slowly became aware of the impact that isolation had on patients, and we attempted to take steps to address these feelings. When feasible we provided emotional support through phone calls or video chats with family members, we tried to arrange for social workers or chaplains to speak with patients, but in many instances, they were reluctant to come to the COVID-19 units. We also encouraged activities such as reading or watching movies to help pass the time.

Death Threats

When the pandemic hit, I was one of the first healthcare professionals in the United States to advocate for the use of masks to prevent the spread of COVID-19. However, this led to me receiving death threats from individuals who were opposed to the idea of wearing masks. I became a target for those who believed that the use of masks was an infringement on their personal freedoms, and my advocacy for masks made me a lightning rod for their anger.

On a midafternoon in June of 2020, I was called emergently by my spouse, Sara. She indicated that she was at my office when they received a phone call from an individual stating *"tell Dr. Varon that he will not be doing his rounds tomorrow as we are going to kill him for his stupid beliefs of masks"*. My wife and office staff were quite scared and concerned about safety. At that point in time in the pandemic, I rarely was going to my office, as I was 100% of my time at the hospital helping those with COVID-19. I told them not to worry, that this was probably just someone unhappy to see me doing so much work and advocating for social distancing and masking. At that time, we really did not know for sure if masks worked or not, but it was common sense to consider their use.

A few days later, several of my social media account, started to have hate messages and death threats. All of them indicated that COVID-19 was not real and that if I kept talking about this illness, I was going to die. Again, I did not pay attention to such threats and continued to do my work and to speak out about the importance of mask-wearing and other measures to combat the spread of the virus. I had recognized that the situation was urgent and that it was critical to do everything possible to slow the spread of the virus and save lives. I remained committed to my patients and the community, even in the face of danger, and continued to put my own health on the line to care for COVID-19 patients.

The threats continued to come. My office got additional phone calls indicating that my *"days were limited"* as I continued to advocate for people to do the right thing. My opinions were based on the information that we had available at that time. Yet, these threats continued. I remember getting to my office at the hospital and receiving an extensive letter asking me to stop all my efforts for COVID-19, as this was a lie and a conspiracy. That day, I officially got concerned and elected to call the then Chief of Houston Police. I had the opportunity to work with him during the first few months of the pandemic, and we had a good working relationship. When I called him, I stated *"Art, I am getting a lot of death threats"*. I recall his response like if it was yesterday. The Chief, in a firm voice said, *"welcome to the club"*. He proceeded to explain to me that these were very common threats that highly visible people get, and there are rarely acted upon. That made me feel better.

These instances continued to occur and slowly disappeared over time. For me, this experience highlights the intense and sometimes dangerous polarization that arose around the issue of masks during the pandemic. Being brave in the face of adversity is a testament to the importance of healthcare professionals who are willing to stand up for their beliefs and do what is right, even when it is unpopular or puts us in harm's way. Several of my friends were in similar situations and just reminds me of the sacrifices made by those on the front lines of the fight against the virus.

911: I Have Been Kidnapped

An 83-year-old woman presented to the emergency department of our hospital complaining of fever and cough for a period of 10 days. She had been in her usual state of good health until she was exposed to a grandchild that had COVID-19. A few days later she began having her symptoms. Upon arrival to the hospital, she was awake, alert, complaining of productive cough and fever. The emergency physician ordered a computed tomography (CT scan) of her chest that revealed pneumonia in both lungs. COVID-19 was confirmed by a rapid test. Her blood work revealed an acute inflammatory process, and her oxygenation to be low. To keep her oxygenation at a reasonable level, we had to start her on high-flow nasal cannula or HFNC (which is a device that provides very large amounts of oxygen through the nose and that is used in hospitals for patients with acute respiratory issues). Therefore, the decision to admit her was reached. When the patient was advised as to the need of admission, she initially refused as she *"did not like hospitals"*. However, after talking with her daughter, she agreed to a short-term hospitalization.

On arrival to the COVID-19 unit the patient got quite upset, after realizing that this was an isolation room, that everyone was wearing PPE and that her only communication with the exterior World was through telephone, as no visitation was allowed. She told her nurse that this was unacceptable. The nurse called her daughter, and again convinced her to stay, as she had a bad case of COVID-19 pneumonia, and her outcome would likely be fatal if she did not stay in the hospital.

The patient was treated with our standard protocol and visited several times a day by me or members of my team. Every time we visited her, she complained that she wanted to go home.

We tried to explain to her that her oxygen levels were too low to safely send her home and that the device (HFNC) she required to keep her oxygenation were impossible to place at home. During every visit she was awake and alert and appeared to be aware of what was going on. I had been concerned that the low oxygen levels that she had suffered prior to admission, could get her mental state altered. Yet, she appeared mentally intact on each one of my visits.

Over the course of several days, the patient's condition deteriorated, and she became increasingly confused and disoriented. Her fever spiked, and she experienced shortness of breath, requiring supplemental oxygen. Eventually, her delirium became so severe that she became convinced that she had been kidnapped and was being held against her will. Her family was understandably concerned and reached out to the healthcare staff for answers. The healthcare staff explained that delirium was a common symptom of COVID-19 and that they were doing everything they could to manage her symptoms. We assured them that she was not in danger and that we were closely monitoring her condition.

Despite these reassurances, our patient remained convinced that she had been kidnapped. She would frequently try to leave her hospital room, insisting that she needed to escape. She became hostile towards the healthcare staff, accusing them of being in on the kidnapping. She refused to take her medications, believing that it was part of a scheme to keep her under control.

Our patient's delirium was a cause of great concern for the healthcare staff in our COVID-19 unit. We recognized that her symptoms were a result of her illness and that we needed to take steps to manage her condition effectively. We began to monitor her more closely, providing one-on-one care to ensure that she did not harm herself or others. We also adjusted her medications to alleviate her delirium symptoms.

On the early morning of her 4th day of her hospital stay, I was told that *"the police and paramedics were in the lobby of the hospital"*. When I inquired why, my staff informed me that apparently, they had received a call on the 911 line that morning indicating that one of the patients was being held against their will and had been kidnapped. It did not take me long to ascertain, who the patient was. I escorted the paramedics and the police into the room of our patient. At that point she was confused, screaming, and telling the officers that she had been *"kidnapped and was being held against her wishes"*. Apparently, she had called 911 and indicated such things. The operator immediately dispatched a team of paramedics and the police. At that point in time, I asked her if she knew where she was and she was not able to respond. Because all our patient were receiving blood thinners during this phase of the pandemic, I immediately ordered a brain scan to make sure she did not have any strokes. The scan was normal. The officers and paramedics left the hospital reassured that she had not been kidnapped.

A couple of hours later we arranged for a videoconference with her daughter to help us manage her concerns. Once the patient spoke with her daughter, her mental state improved significantly. She was less disoriented. We made sure that she would be in communication with her daughter several times a day and kept a sitter by her bedside.

After several days of treatment, we were able to wean her from oxygen and was able to be discharged home in stable condition. Upon follow up in our clinic, she was quite apologetic about calling 911 to report such a crime.

Delirium is a common symptom of COVID-19, particularly in older patients or those with pre-existing medical conditions. The cause of delirium in COVID-19 patients is not entirely understood, but it is believed to be related to the body's response to the virus. COVID-19 can cause inflammation throughout the body, including in the brain, which can lead to changes in brain function and behavior. The treatment for delirium in COVID-19 patients is primarily focused on managing the symptoms and addressing any underlying medical conditions that may be contributing to the delirium. Medications, such as antipsychotics and sedatives, may be used to help alleviate the symptoms of delirium, although these medications must be used with caution to avoid adverse side effects. Non-pharmacological interventions, such as music therapy, physical therapy, and social interaction, may also be used to help manage delirium symptoms.

It is Too Hot in Here

No matter what time of the year it was, during the pandemic, it seemed that the COVID-19 unit was always extremely hot. We had a negative pressure system applied to all the rooms, and in addition we used to wear the PPE that kept us warmer. The patients also complained of similar concerns such as the case of a 43-year-old lady who was admitted to the hospital with COVID-19 and severe respiratory distress. She had a history of diabetes, high blood pressure and was morbidly obese. On arrival to our unit, she was placed on assisted ventilation as she was critically ill.

For the next several days she was treated with a variety of medications, and after 6 days we were able to get her of the assisted respirator. After a couple of days, she was able to talk, and we started the physical therapy that was required to start moving her and walking.

On hospital day 12th, on my daily morning rounds, my team and I went to see the patient. Upon entering her room, we found her totally naked. When we asked her why she was naked, she stated *"it is too hot in here"*. Her body temperature was within normal limits and the room temperature was at 70 degrees Fahrenheit (21 Centigrade). At the time, we considered the possibility that either hormonal changes or the medications (in particular, steroids) were culprit.

Over the next 3 days, every time any member of our team went to see the patient, she was totally naked, and continued to give the same response that she had given us before, as to why she was wearing no clothes. We reviewed again her medication list, as well as repeated hormonal work up in hopes of determining why she "felt so hot" all the time. We found no explanation for her symptoms until one late evening, when we "opened" the food she had ordered to be delivered to the hospital and found several energy drinks that she had been using since she was able to resume her food intake. Apparently, she would take 2-3 energy drinks with each meal, as she had been told by "a friend" that this would allow her to lose weight fast.

At that point, we instructed the patient not to have such energy beverages any longer, and this was followed by a complete resolution of her symptoms, as well as the need to have her clothes removed.

She was discharged to her home after 19 days in the hospital in good condition. Upon follow up in our COVID clinic a few weeks later, she indicated that she no longer consumed energy drinks, and that she was on a medically controlled diet to lose weight.

I can recall, like countless of my colleagues around the world, facing the intense heat and discomfort in the COVID-19 unit. Most of it was related to wearing personal protective equipment (PPE). The challenges we encountered while working in the COVID-19 unit were not only emotionally and mentally draining but physically demanding as well. The image at the end of this chapter of me emerging from the unit, drenched in sweat after just one hour inside, paints a vivid picture of the arduous conditions we faced.

The PPE required for healthcare workers in COVID units consisted of multiple layers, including a gown, gloves, mask, goggles, and often a face shield. These layers were crucial in preventing the spread of the virus but also create a stifling environment for those wearing them. The combination of heat, limited airflow, and the body's natural response to stress lead to profuse sweating.

Within minutes of entering the unit, healthcare providers experienced a surge of heat trapped within their protective gear.

As we attended to patients, the physical exertion only exacerbated the situation. The intense heat generated by our own bodies, coupled with the insulation provided by the PPE, was overwhelming. It was not uncommon for healthcare workers to lose several pounds of body weight due to excessive sweating during their shifts.

Dueling Cardiac Arrests

As an Acute Care (Critical Care, Emergency Medicine) specialist, I am used to deal with a variety of life-or-death situations at the same time. However, during the pandemic, these circumstances intensified to the point where multiple casualties would occur simultaneously and the healthcare providers would run from room-to-room. This was one of those circumstances.

During the peak of the Delta variant, we had instances where our little hospital (a total of 114 beds) was completely full of COVID-19 patients. At some point in time, I had 88 patients who were critically ill. I was the only critical care physician working on their case. The amount of work that this constituted made me stay up to 20 continuous hours in the hospital and on several occasion, I would stay for days at a time.

On one of those days, close to noon time, I was asked to see a patient who had been admitted overnight and who was "not doing well". He was a 34-year-old gentleman without any significant past medical history that had 3 weeks of symptoms and had deteriorated to the point where he was admitted to our COVID-19 unit. As I ran to see him, I found out that he had been infected with COVID-19 for approximately 3 weeks. He knew he was "positive" for the virus but had refused to go to the hospital. This was not uncommon. At that time, patients had 3 reasons not to seek hospital care for COVID-19: Some believed that going to the hospital meant they would die (which was not completely untrue as it was a time where the average mortality rate for patients admitted with such illness was in excess of 40%). Fortunately, in our hospital, at the time, we only had a reported mortality of 4.4% utilizing several protocols that we developed utilizing Food and Drug Administration (FDA)-approved medications that were being repurposed. Second, other patients were concerned about the financial implications that being admitted to the hospital would have, and finally, many did not want to come to medical institutions as they were concerned about the "stigma" that having COVID-19 had at the time (very similar to the one patients with AIDS had in the 1980s).

As I approached the bed of this young man, his oxygenation was below survival. At that point, I instructed my crew to provide me with the necessary items to intubate (insert a tube into his throat), so I could connect him to a mechanical respirator. This man was dying and had to save his life. Despite placing the tube and connecting him to a respirator, his oxygenation continued to drop. X-rays and blood work were being done when we lost his pulse. He was in a cardiac arrest. My team assumed their positions to provide full cardiopulmonary resuscitation (CPR).

CPR during COVID-19 was extremely difficult, as we were wearing the PPEs and that made the rescuers sweat more than the usual. The fatigue of the healthcare providers increased exponentially. As we were trying to save this man's life, I could see the members of my team sweat nonstop and get short winded. The young man was not responding to the efforts in the first 5 minutes of resuscitation. Suddenly, while directing the CPR efforts, one of the nurses from another patient that was several rooms away, came into the room screaming *"the patient in room X just developed a cardiac arrest"*. I was not expecting this scenario. I had the life of a young man in my hands, when suddenly someone else's life was at stake as well.

The other patient was a morbidly obese 57-year-old lady with multiple prior medical problems, that had been admitted to our unit 10 days prior to this episode. She had been placed on a ventilator as her oxygenation was terrible. In the day prior to this event, her oxygen levels improved, and we were hopeful she soon would not require such lifesaving therapy. Apparently, as my other patient was fighting for his life, this lady suddenly became pulseless, the nurses ran to her bedside to offer resuscitation maneuvers. We were already short-staffed as many of our nurses had fallen ill with COVID-19. I left the young man with resuscitation efforts in progress to run to the aid of this other lady.

Upon my arrival to her room, there were two nurses administering CPR. She had a complete flat line on the monitor. 2 additional members of my team came with me and helped the nurses with these maneuvers.

I had to think fast. Two patients. Two cardiac arrests. One exhausted critical care physician. Which one to attend to? How fast to run back to the other one? These were the thoughts running thru my mind. Yet, both patients were equally ill, and I needed to save them both. No matter what. So, I ended up running back and forth from one room, on one end of the hallway, to the other one and try to help both. CPR was continued on both patients by the team, while I was giving order after order of medications to be administered.

The young man had a return of his pulse after approximately 10 minutes of CPR. Rather than staying and celebrating this success, I ran back to see the other patient, who was still undergoing CPR. On my return to her room, the nurses were visibly exhausted, and we were not getting any results. She still had a complete flat line. I asked one of the members of the team to get hold of her husband, so I could let him know what was going on. As soon as I was able to explain to the spouse that her condition was critical, he requested to continue the resuscitation efforts until he was able to get hold of his adult children and explain what was going on. CPR continued on her. I rapidly went to the other room to check on the newly resuscitated man and made sure that appropriate tests and imaging studies were being conducted.

By the time I went back to the lady with a cardiac arrest, 28 minutes had elapsed since we started CPR. In my experience, adult patients with normal temperature, rarely survive after 20 minutes of resuscitative efforts. A few minutes later, her husband called us back and requested to stop all resuscitation, as her spouse had been quite clear that she did not want to have such interventions, if we thought her chances of meaningful survival were small. At that point, I stopped the rescuers from continuing CPR, and I pronounced her dead.

I went back to check on the younger individual. He was still critically ill, but at least he had a pulse. Over the next 24 hours his condition improved. We found that the reason for his sudden deterioration had been a large blood clot in the vessels that feed the lungs, even though he had been on blood thinners. I elected to proceed with a procedure where he received a "clot buster" inside the affected vessel. He improved dramatically. A few days later, I was able to wean him off the ventilator.

After almost 3 weeks in the hospital, this man was able to go home totally intact. On follow up he has had no further issues. This time we saved one, but we had also lost one life. Yet, we had to try.

These 2 patients had what I call "dueling cardiac arrests", also known as co-arrests or simultaneous cardiac arrests, which refer to a rare, but potentially deadly scenario, where two or more individuals experience cardiac arrest at the same time and in the same location. In such cases, healthcare providers assess the situation and prioritize treatment based on the severity of each individual's condition. Dueling cardiac arrests present a unique challenge for healthcare providers, as they must determine which patient to treat first and how to best allocate limited resources. This was even worse in the context of COVID-19.

At the peak of the pandemic, healthcare providers were faced with difficult choices when a patient had a cardiac arrest.

Due to the risk of transmitting the virus, healthcare providers had to weigh the benefits of performing CPR against the potential risk of infection to themselves and others. In some cases, healthcare providers made the difficult decision not to perform CPR, as they did not want to use critical resources that were needed to care for other patients. Many of my colleagues would not even initiate CPR in these settings. A serious concern many clinicians had was that during the peak of the pandemic we were faced with a shortage of personal protective equipment (PPE), including gloves, gowns, and masks. This shortage made it challenging for healthcare providers to safely perform CPR on patients who were suspected or confirmed to have COVID-19. Additionally, the act of performing CPR generates aerosols, which can spread the virus to others in the room. This placed healthcare providers at an increased risk of infection and put others in the room, including other patients and staff members, at risk as well. In some cases, we made the difficult decision not to perform CPR on patients with COVID-19, even though it is a standard life-saving intervention. Instead, we focused on providing other forms of support, such as oxygen therapy and medications, to help stabilize the patient when feasible. This decision was not taken lightly, and healthcare providers knew that it could mean the difference between life and death for some patients.

These difficult choices were particularly challenging for healthcare providers, who are trained to do everything in their power to save a patient's life. The frustration of not being able to help a patient was beyond words. The decision not to perform CPR was especially difficult for healthcare providers who were working in areas with high mortality rates, such as intensive care units and emergency departments. They had to make these decisions while also dealing with the emotional toll of seeing many patients die from the virus.

I Miss My Wife on Thanksgiving

Of all the patients that I admitted to the hospital during the pandemic, this one is very close to my heart. The picture on the cover of this book depicts my patient and I, and this picture went viral all over the World.

On the morning of Thanksgiving day 2020, I was doing my usual rounds at looking at all the patients and reviewing the data with my team. Rounds usually consisted of extensive review of the last 24 hours of vital signs, laboratories, and imaging as well as a close examination of the patients in their rooms. On this occasion, I had with me Mr. Go Nakamura, a famous freelance photographer that had requested permission from the hospital to follow me and take pictures of situations that would depict what was going on in the COVID-19 unit without violating patient privacy. The hospital granted such permission and Mr. Nakamura came that day to follow me during my activities. As I was walking through the unit, Mr. Nakamura would take pictures of what was going on with the discussions with the team and other pertinent images. We would not "pose" for the camera, and he would do his job very discretely to the point where we would not even know he was there.

The nurses and the rest of my team had prepared a variety of dishes to "celebrate" Thanksgiving, as we all knew we were going to stay in the hospital all day long. We had multiple critically ill patients, and we were very busy. However, I wanted to round efficiently, so that the team could spend a few minutes eating food prepared for such occasion.

We saw the first 4 patients in a relatively short period of time. As I was approaching the next room, I encountered a 78-year-old gentleman that had been admitted to the hospital 3 days prior to Thanksgiving with shortness of breath, fever, cough, a positive COVID-19 test and radiographic imaging consistent with severe pneumonia. This fragile man had a reasonable medical history and had been admitted due to concerns of worsening of the pneumonia. For the next two days after admission, he had been pleasant, oriented, and following all the instructions given to him by the staff. He had been connected to the continuous cardiac monitor, placed on oxygen and received the medications that were part of our COVID-19 "cocktail".

On Thanksgiving, when I entered his room, I found him standing by his bedside, completely disconnected from his monitor and his oxygen, and crying. Yes, this gentleman was crying, and I did not know why. I had no idea if he was in pain or if he was upset. I approached him and asked him *"why are you crying?"*. As I asked this question, he looked at me, all covered in my PPE and responded, *"Today is Thanksgiving and I miss my wife"*. He was alone in the hospital room, surrounded by beeping machines, sterile walls, and white bedsheets. He missed his wife terribly, and the thought of spending Thanksgiving alone made him feel even more isolated. Can you imagine how I felt? The fact that this elderly gentleman wanted to be with his wife during Thanksgiving, and he couldn't because he was in the hospital, and we had strict orders to prohibit anyone from entering the hospital that was not a patient. He truly broke my heat. At that time, I did not care about COVID-19, I did not even think about the risk of getting infected. I just went ahead and hugged him as hard as I could! This man needed compassion. What I did not know, was that Mr. Go Nakamura was close to me capturing with his camera this moment.

After a few minutes of a good hug and convincing him into sitting in his bed, I called his spouse and we all spoke on the phone. He felt better, and I could tell he was going to be compliant with the therapeutic interventions we had. He was hooked back to the monitor and oxygen. I decided to stay by his bedside longer and we spoke about a variety of topics. He smiled. Once I was sure he was better emotionally, I continued my rounds and my rest of my Thanksgiving working day.

The next morning, I came early to the hospital and as soon as I started reviewing the data of several patients, I begin receiving a series of phone calls from a variety of media outlets that wanted to talk to me about the *"photo"*. I had no idea of what they were talking about. They kept mentioning a picture that was circulating on the net of me hugging a patient. To be perfectly honest, this was not the first patient I had hugged, but I never thought that Mr. Nakamura had taken a photograph that captured the most amazing expression of medical humanity. Such image circulated virally on the internet, and I had dozens of interviews in the days to follow regarding the events that lead to such momentum. Some inquired if this had been "staged". Others really cared about this gentleman and what was going on with him. I received hundreds of letters from all over the World from people that saw the image and wanted to thank me for showing the "caring" side of medicine.

Over the next few days, this lonely man felt better, and we were able to send him home to the care of his spouse. I followed him several times in the months to follow and to date, I continue to talk to his spouse. Of note, Mr. Nakamura's picture won several awards and has become an icon of several medical illustrations.

The photographic image quickly became a symbol of the dedication and compassion shown by healthcare workers on the front lines of the COVID-19 pandemic. It highlighted the emotional toll of caring for patients with a highly contagious and deadly virus, as well as the human connection that can be so important in times of crisis. The picture also sparked conversations about the importance of empathy and compassion in healthcare, particularly during a global pandemic. It raised awareness about the challenges faced by healthcare workers and the need for support and resources to help them cope with the stresses of their jobs. Furthermore, the picture served as a reminder of the severity of the COVID-19 pandemic and the toll it had taken on individuals and communities around the world. It highlighted the importance of following public health guidelines such as wearing masks and practicing social distancing to help prevent the spread of the virus and reduce the burden on healthcare workers.

For me, this image had significant implications in terms of highlighting the emotional toll of the pandemic on healthcare workers and the importance of empathy, compassion, and public health measures in preventing the spread of the virus.

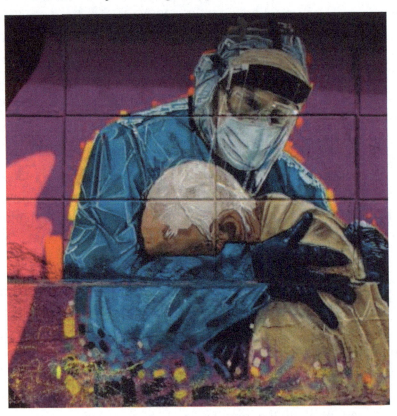

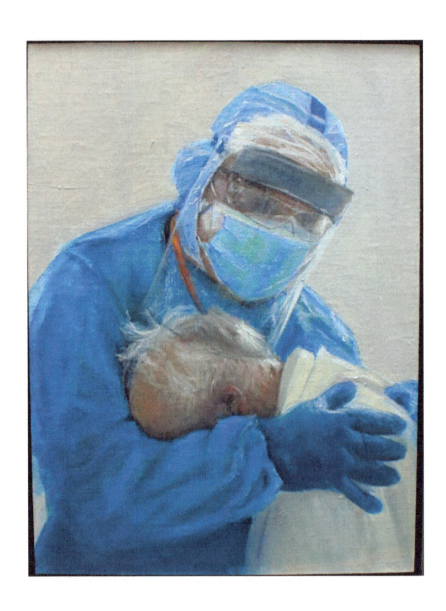

The Family that Bleeds Too Much

As mentioned before, during the pandemic, it was a common occurrence to admit couples and sometimes, entire families to the hospital with acute COVID-19 pneumonia. Some of them critically ill, others with milder symptoms. The fact is that it was not uncommon to have several members of the same family hospitalized in our unit.

During late 2020, we received a family consisting of a 76-year-old mother and her 2 sons (38 and 42 years of age, respectively). They all had been suffering with COVID-19 symptoms for 2 weeks prior to arrival to our hospital. The mother was previously healthy, and was complaining of severe shortness of breath, cough, fever, and chest pain. Her chest x-ray revealed severe pneumonia and COVID-19 testing confirmed the diagnosis. Based on very low oxygen levels, and her unstable vital signs noted in the emergency department, the decision to admit her followed.

The 38- year-old son had been complaining of cough for two weeks, and in the 24 hours prior to admission, he had been coughing up blood. His oxygenation was borderline, and he was admitted to our COVID-19 unit as well. Additional testing and imaging confirmed that he had also a case of severe COVID-19 pneumonia. We found no evidence of any prior bleeding disorder on him and assumed that the blood that he was coughing was related to the severe irritation of the airways that the virus created.

The last member of this family, a 42-year-old gentleman with a history of poorly controlled diabetes, had similar symptoms as his mother and brother but was not coughing up any blood. His chest x-ray also demonstrated pneumonia and his COVID-19 test was positive. He was admitted to the hospital. Because of overcrowding of the rooms, we could not assign his bed to the room where his brother was staying.

All the members of this hospitalized family underwent further diagnostic testing and received our standard therapy consisting of vitamins, steroid and blood thinner. We were using blood thinners in all patients (even in the ones coughing up blood) as we had seen that the risk of clots in the vessels feeding the lungs were extremely high and this was a lethal complication that needed prevention.

On day 3 of hospitalization, I was called to the room of the senior member of this family. The lady was complaining of severe left breast pain and had visibly enlarged the left side of her chest. When I touched the area, she was in severe pain. According to the patient and the nurse, she developed the sudden chest pain and increase in breast size without any precipitating factors. I ordered an immediate computed tomography (CT) scan of her chest that revealed she had a new, large area of bleeding inside her left breast. This was the first time in the pandemic that I had seen such event. I requested to immediately stop all the blood thinners.

That same day both adult children of this lady had also bleeding issues. The younger one began having large amounts of blood in the urine, whereas his older brother was continuing to have a lot of blood in his phlegm. They both required higher amount of oxygen as this was occurring. Although they both were "relatively stable", I got concerned that these family members were all having bleeding complications, which we had not seen to this extent in the prior hundreds of patients that we had admitted during the pandemic.

After careful review of their medication administration and laboratory values, I found no evidence of any wrongdoing or excess in therapy. Additional laboratory investigations revealed that all these members of this unique family had a special enzyme deficiency that made them more prone towards bleeding. According to them, this was the first instance in their lives.

Once the blood thinners were discontinued, all of them had their "active bleeding stop". The mother had less pain and with time her large bruise subsided, and she was discharged home in stable conditions on hospital day 11. Both brothers had slower recoveries due to the amount of oxygen that they required. They had no further bleeding complications and went home on day 12 after admission. All 3 members of this family were seen in follow up in the post COVID-19 clinic and had no further episodes of bleeding.

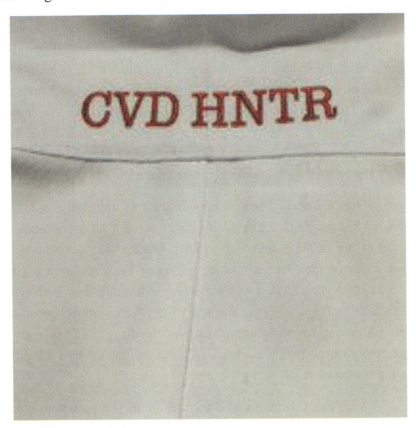

I Want a Donut

During the pandemic, we spend countless hours in the COVID-19 unit caring for dozens of patients at a time. In many instances, I would not eat for a complete day. Many of our patients were aware of how hard we were working, and in many instances, they would ask their family members to bring us food. At some point in time, we were overwhelmed with the number of families that would bring us a variety of foods. Most of them were "non healthy", but we did not care, as we were all starving.

One day, the spouse of one of the TV reporters that had come to the unit to understand how we worked, sent us several boxes of donuts. You must know, that "I love donuts" and, unfortunately, I do not know how to eat only one. So, receiving several boxes of donuts really made my day. I was so happy of this occurrence that I kept on telling my patients about it, as I did my daily rounds.

I went to see a 42-year-old lady that we had admitted with severe COVID-19 pneumonia that had required to be placed on a machine that provides oxygen and pressure without the need to place a tube in the throat. Such device, called BiPAP, allows the body to get oxygenation, but must be kept attached to the face via a very specific mask. Our patient was compliant with the use of such device, and she was allowed to remove such device a couple of times a day for short periods of time, so she could have some small meals with very strict nursing supervision. This lady was progressing well, and I was quite optimistic she would do well. After I had examined her, I told her that she was doing well and that I expected she would be off the BiPAP device in the next 48 hours. I then proceeded to tell her how happy I was with my "donuts" that day. She immediately, tried to tell me something, but because of the mask, I could not understand what she was saying, so I offered her a piece of paper and a pen, so she could write what she was asking me.

As I gave the piece of paper and pen to the patient, and expecting she would ask something about her condition, or the BiPAP, I got shocked when I saw her message: *"I want a donut"*.

This lady was critically ill, and her only request for me was that she wanted a donut! You must understand that most of my patients at the time had no taste, and many of them were not interested in food. For me, to see that a patient was specifically asking for a donut was something quite unique. So, I decided to get out of the unit, pick up a donut, and came right back to the patient. I then proceeded to remove the BiPAP device of the patient, and place her on the high flow nasal canula, while observing her levels of oxygen and other vital signs and I sat with her and watched her eat the donut. I must say that I also brought a donut for myself, and we both enjoyed it very much.

The facial expression that my patient had when I brought her the donut made me extremely happy. This lady was quite ill, yet there was something that I could do in between this medical chaos to make her happy.

As the days went on, this lady was able to come off her BiPAP device, and slowly progressed to the point where she no longer required oxygen and was able to be sent home. I have been following her since that day in my outpatient clinic, and every time she comes to see me, she brings me a box of donuts.

The Music Video

The COVID-19 pandemic presented an unprecedented challenge for healthcare workers all over the world. All those brave men and women were on the frontlines, risking their lives every day to save the lives of others. So how could we thank them in a simple way in the middle of the pandemic? My good friend Ken Freirich had an answer: Write and produce a song and video for healthcare workers! I never would have imagined this song and video would play every day in our unit, motivating my team and me to get through the long and difficult days and nights.

This idea started when Ken, an entrepreneur, songwriter, drummer and philanthropist, was on a happy hour Zoom with his employees on Good Friday 2020. At the time, Ken was CEO of Health Monitor Network, the largest patient education/engagement company in the United States, known for publications and exam room digital posters. (We have the digital screens in our offices).

Since Ken and Health Monitor worked with so many healthcare professionals like me, he wanted to help in some way. And now, during this time of crisis, he felt a calling to write and produce a song that could bring people together. During that Good Friday Zoom he announced to employees that he was going to write and produce a song that would serve as an anthem to healthcare workers. The next day, in just six hours, Ken wrote the lyrics to *Healthcare Workers Rock!* and the song and movement was born.

Moved by the opportunity to help others and his love of music, Ken started a new record label, Better World Records, and established a new artist name,

Random Acts of Kindness, to deliver his music to the world.

By August 2020, he had produced and released the first version of *Healthcare Workers Rock!*, but after receiving feedback from the music press about the need to raise its production quality, he decided to do a remix, bringing in a world-class team to help him. Serving as executive producer, Ken recruited P!nk drummer Mark Schulman to play drums, GRAMMY Award-winning producer and mixer Scott Jacoby to produce and remix the song and GRAMMY-Award winner Emily Lazar to master the track.

I remember being contacted one afternoon by Ken, who told me he was going to create a video for Healthcare Workers Rock! and would love for me to participate. He was enthusiastic about bringing the music to life through video and wanted to do something more for those of us who were working non-stop in a difficult environment. His vision was to share real stories of both healthcare workers and patients with the world. He wanted to highlight the incredibly brave people who were risking their lives every day to help others and the patients/families impacted by COVID. The idea sounded amazing. The question was, how to do this during COVID with so many logistical challenges?

Ken promptly sent me the lyrics of the song, which I loved when I saw them. I remember telling Ken, "The truth is healthcare workers are at their breaking point. The stress of the pandemic right now is unbearable. The music and lyrics of *Healthcare Worker's Rock!* gives us an emotional release that makes every day more tolerable. "

Now I had to convince my team that it was time to do something fun that could feature them, but they would have to learn the lyrics, and maybe even sing! Can you imagine the idea of shooting a music video in the middle of chaos in the hospital? For me, it made perfect sense, as it would allow my staff to have a team-building experience that was unique. Yet, this would be a very difficult task.

Ken was very generous and hired a professional video crew to film the music video onsite. I obtained consent from our hospital that would allow the film crew to enter the COVID-19 unit under strict compliance circumstances to make sure no patients would be recorded without their specific consent and be fully protected in PPE. In the meanwhile, I shared the lyrics with my entire staff and told them about the project. It was interesting that everyone was excited to participate. Despite their exhaustion, they were happy to do something to improve the morale of the unit. I had a nurse cry when she was asked to be in the video because it reinforced what a difference, she was making for so many.

The day the video crew showed up everyone was very excited. The healthcare workers who participated in the *Healthcare Workers Rock!* video were filled with energy and excitement. Many of them had been working long hours and dealing with the stress and challenges of caring for patients during the COVID-19 pandemic. But on this day, they were able to come together and take part in a fun and uplifting project that celebrated their work and dedication. As they arrived at our hospital, where the video was being shot, the healthcare workers were greeted with music and smiles. They were given colorful props and wore their PPEs, and they danced and sang along to the upbeat Healthcare Workers Rock! song. Despite the physical and emotional toll of their work, they were able to let loose and have fun, enjoying the sense of community and support that the project provided.

Throughout the day, the healthcare workers showed incredible enthusiasm and spirit, performing their dance routines with passion and joy. They were proud to represent their profession and to be a part of a project that recognized their hard work and sacrifice. As the shoot wrapped up, they left feeling energized and inspired, with a renewed sense of purpose and appreciation for their work as healthcare workers.

As it turned out, Ken also sent the crew to film the family of his good friend, Houston hometown hero Rodney Hampton. One of the greatest NY Giants running backs of all time, Rodney was a Super Bowl Champion and had been to the Pro Bowl twice. As big supporters of healthcare workers, the Hamptons were thrilled to participate in the video.

The music video had a lot of success, becoming a rallying cry for healthcare workers worldwide and a reminder that their efforts were not going unnoticed. It also raised awareness of the daily struggles healthcare workers faced, such as long hours, lack of protective equipment and stress.

The completed video and song played in our unit day in and day out. As I witnessed our workers humming and singing the song to help lift their own spirits and the spirits of others, I knew the song and the video were just what the doctor ordered. I wanted to help get this music therapy to every hospital around the world because it provided the boost that kept healthcare workers going.

In addition to the music video, Ken and his team launched a website, *healthcareworkersrock.org*. The *Healthcare Workers Rock!* video was an example of one of the many random acts of kindness during the pandemic. One of the most remarkable things about the video was the way it brought people together. The collaboration between songwriters, producers, musicians and healthcare professionals was a testament to the power of creativity and community in times of crisis. The video also moved other artists to create their own tributes to healthcare workers, from paintings and murals to other musical performances.

The Healthcare Workers Rock music video and website are a powerful reminder of the bravery and dedication of healthcare workers during the COVID-19 pandemic.

For more information about the song and video please visit: Randomactsofkindnessmusic.com or healthcareworkersrock.org

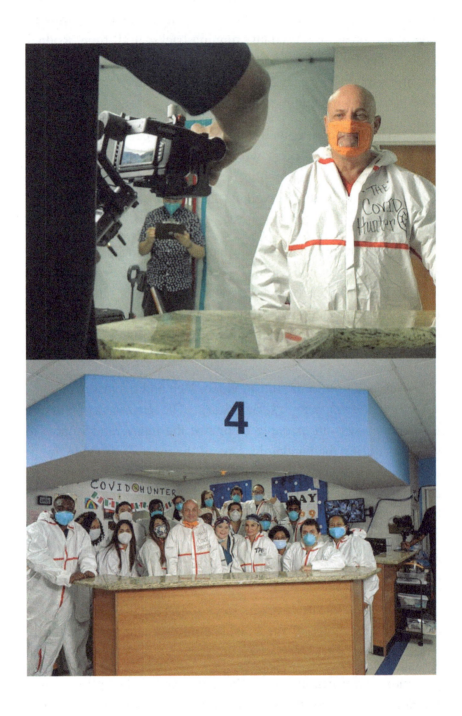

Photos: © Better World Records, LLC, 2020. All rights reserved.

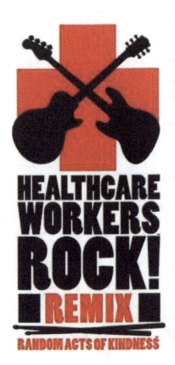 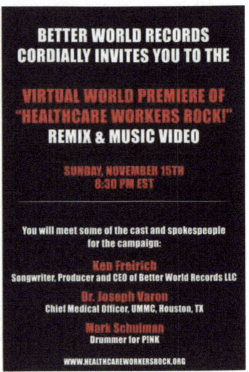

Healthcare Workers Rock! Lyrics

Written by Ken Freirich

© 2020 Better World Records LLC

VERSE 1

We are on the frontline

Putting ourselves in danger

Trying to save the lives

Of oh so many strangers

Don't look at them as numbers

That's not what you mean to us

We're brothers, sisters, mothers

Like family, it's all worth the fuss

PRECHORUS

This is what we do

Day in and day out

This is what we do

And we just wanna shout

CHORUS

Healthcare Workers Rock!

Working 'round the clock

Strong and courageous, never gonna stop

Won't give up, won't give in

Cause we have got to win

Let's Rock!

VERSE 2

Never seen a thing like this

In my whole career

The battle's really tough

Feels like more than a year

Supplies are getting short

Still we try to make the best

One day at a time

'Cause we can never rest

PRECHORUS

This is what we do

Day in and day out

This is what we do

And we just wanna shout

CHORUS

Healthcare Workers Rock!

Working 'round the clock

Strong and courageous, never gonna stop

Won't give up, won't give in

Cause we have got to win

BRIDGE

It's time we all remember

The real heroes are at home

Our partners, daughters and sons

We miss each and every one

VERSE 3

The world needs us now

So we are standing strong

Putting patients first

All day and all night long

We will make it through

One way or the other

Stay true to the cause

Caring for one another

PRECHORUS

This is what we do

Day in and day out

This is what we do

And we just wanna shout

CHORUS

Healthcare Workers Rock!

Working 'round the clock

Strong and courageous, never gonna stop

Won't give up, won't give in

Cause we have got to win

CHORUS

Healthcare Workers Rock!

Working 'round the clock

Strong and courageous, never gonna stop

Won't give up, won't give in

Cause we have got to win

Let's Rock!

Can I Have Double Portions?

One of the characteristic findings that I had among patients being admitted to our unit, was that most of them were not interested in eating too much. This was mostly because, COVID-19, affected their taste buds and smell receptors. Therefore, food was basically tasteless to them. This was something that we would see every single day.

On a late afternoon in March of 2021, I was called to see a 33-year-old woman that had been admitted to the COVID-19 unit with severe pneumonia, oxygenation issues and acute kidney disease. She was an obese lady with history of diabetes and high blood pressure that was non-compliant with her medications or doctor's visits. She had symptoms for 2 weeks prior to admission, but refused to come into the hospital, as she had the concern that she would be carefully supervised about her diet.

On arrival to the COVID-19 unit, she was in distress, complaining of shortness of breath despite oxygen that was being given via a face mask. Her blood pressure was high, and her blood sugar was 3 times the upper limit of normal. She was started on our standard protocol for patients in such condition. Additionally, we asked a kidney specialist to see her, as her kidney function was bad, most likely related to her poor compliance with her diabetes and blood pressure medications. In addition, a careful nutritional assessment and diet counseling was requested as her body mass index (a person's weight in kilograms or pounds, divided by the square of height in meters or feet), was almost twice the normal for someone her age and gender.

On the morning after her admission, the nursing staff indicated that this lady had food delivered twice overnight and that she had refused to eat the hospital food. It is not uncommon that patients refuse to eat hospital food, however in this case, the diet prescribed was necessary to prevent any further blood sugar elevation and worsening kidney function. Yet, the patient had elected not to follow the instructions. I decided to talk to the patient in length about the importance of compliance, her clinical condition, and the fact, that at the time we had to optimize her in order to save her life. She was "apologetic" and stated that this would not happen again. I proceeded to work on my other patients and continued my day in the unit.

That afternoon I was called back to her room. The patient was screaming, removing her oxygen mask, and demanding that she wanted a large pepperoni pizza. On my arrival to her room, I could see a visibly agitated lady screaming profanities, as apparently, her family had ordered a pizza to be delivered to the hospital, but the nurses had intercepted it at the nurses' station, so she would not eat it, and increase her chances of getting in trouble. A call had been made to the family members to indicate the importance of compliance, and not to aid the patient in getting food from the outside. She was awake, alert and knew what was going on. Her oxygen levels were reasonable, despite she removing her mask on and off. She was physically abusive against the healthcare providers around her to the point that security was called in to assist in calming her down.

As I approached her, she was already sitting on a bedside chair. I convinced her to place her oxygen mask back on her face and started a conversation in hopes to diffuse the situation. She was clearly upset as she stated we were *"stealing her food"*. She also mentioned that she was *"a big girl and needed a lot more food than the one she was receiving"*. I discussed with her the mortality data that we had for COVID-19 at the time. The fact that obesity was an indicator of mortality in many cases. Also, the fact that her kidney function was not normal and that some foods had high levels of potassium and that could literally kill her. The conversation was evolving well, and she was much more relaxed. I was quite happy of my performance as a communicator, until she looked at me straight into my eyes (as I was in full PPE) and said, *"can I have double portions?"*. At that point, my feeling of being a good communicator rapidly dissipated! Clearly, I was not making it clear that she had a serious problem and that we had to work together to prevent further issues. I had to think of a way in which I could convince this lady to allow me to help her. This was going to be a monumental task based on what I had just witnessed.

At that time, I decided that oxygenation was more important that fighting for food. I would allow the patient to have double portions for the next 24 hours as a "peace offering". I wanted her to trust me. I would have to increase her insulin dosing. I also made another call to her family and explained the importance of compliance. They agreed to follow my instructions and avoid sending food to the patient.

By the fifth hospital day, she was doing much better and was on minimal among of oxygen via a nasal cannula. She was very pleasant with the healthcare providers since she had received her double portions of food. At that point we spoke about cutting down on the calories and the benefits of a low-carbohydrate diet. She appeared to be responsive to the idea. Time would tell if she would comply. The next day, she was discharged home to follow up in our outpatient COVID-19 clinic. She never came back.

In most of my patients with COVID-19, hunger was never an issue, yet this illness can affect a patient's appetite, and they may feel hungrier than usual, like in this patient's case. This could be due to a variety of reasons, such as the body using more energy to fight off the infection or changes in taste and smell. In addition, being in isolation and dealing with a serious illness can be emotionally taxing, and some patients may turn to food for comfort.

Let's Camp by the Window

The COVID-19 pandemic brought significant changes to the way we interact with others, especially in settings such as hospitals. These settings were forced to implement strict visitation policies to prevent the spread of the virus and, many families were unable to visit their loved ones in person. To stay connected, some families resorted to camping outside the hospital window of their loved ones. This practice involved setting up a makeshift campsite outside the hospital and spending long hours looking through the window at their loved one, often holding up signs or speaking to them on the phone.

On December 2020, I admitted to our COVID-19 unit a 79-year-old gentleman with history of heart disease, diabetes and high blood pressure that had been found unconscious by a family member. He was transported to the emergency department, where on arrival, he was lethargic, with an elevated fever and a very low oxygen level. The emergency physician, immediately attended to him and ordered a variety of diagnostic tests that had confirmed the diagnosis. This man had severe COVID-19 pneumonia, with dangerously low oxygen levels. This illness had progressed into a state of shock that required aggressive use of intravenous medications to keep his blood pressure stable and the aid of a mechanical ventilator to support his respirations. His condition was critical on arrival with limited chances of survival based on his prior medical conditions as well as the severity of the viral illness.

I spoke with the family as soon as the patient arrived to the unit and I was able to assess him in full. They were extremely upset that they were not allowed to come inside the hospital to spend time with the patient, due to the rules that the County Judge had established for healthcare facilities in our area. The son became verbally abusive, but eventually calmed down. I told him what room had been assigned for his father, and that I would try to do videoconferencing from his room later in the day.

A few hours later I was called by the security team of the hospital, as apparently the family (at least 12 members) had come to the hospital grounds and had set up tents outside the patient's room. I went outside the hospital to verify the information. To my surprise, this family had placed two 4 person tents outside the window of the patient's room.

While what this family did by camping outside the hospital window may seem extreme, for many families, such action provided a sense of comfort and connection during such a difficult time. The isolation that came with the COVID-19 restrictions, was particularly challenging for patients who were already struggling with illness or injury, such as in this case. By being present outside the hospital, families provided emotional support and reassurance to their loved ones, even if they were not able to be physically close to them. For families, the act of camping outside a hospital window also provided a sense of urgency, in a situation that often made them feel helpless.

The patient continued to deteriorate in the next 48 hours despite maximum medical support. While I was hopeful that our therapy could abort the process, I also knew that this was an uphill battle and I had his family literally looking from the window, from their "camp".

On the early afternoon of the fifth hospital day, security called me again to come and see this family one more time, as they were being aggressive. I came over to the area where they had installed to find out that now, they had a full barbeque grill and were grilling hamburgers and hotdogs. Indeed, it appeared more to be a family gathering rather than vigilant members wanting to have a constant update on his condition. The security guard and I spoke to them and asked them to remove their grill due to the proximity with the main oxygen line to the hospital and the risk of an explosion. It took some time to convince them, but eventually they took such cooking apparatus away. From that day onwards, I had meetings with this family twice a day to update them on the patient's condition. After 11 days of hospitalization and, despite maximum medical therapy, our patient expired. Two of the family members were allowed to come inside the unit with full PPE, to say their goodbyes to this unfortunate gentleman.

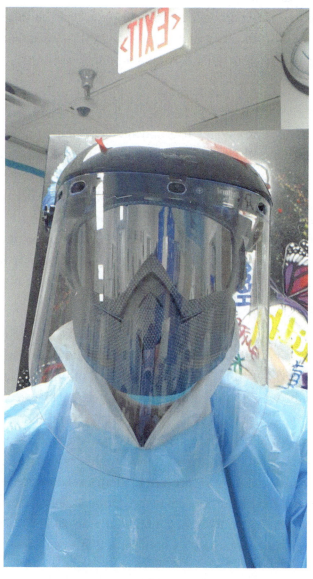

The Escape Artist

An escape artist is a performer who specializes in escaping from restraints or confinement. They use various techniques to break free from handcuffs, ropes, chains, straitjackets, and other devices that would typically be used to restrain a person. Some escape artists perform their stunts on stage as part of a magic or variety show, while others perform daring escapes in public places or on television. In the context of the COVID-19 pandemic, these escape artists became quite common among these units.

Early in the pandemic, we admitted a 38-year-old lady with severe COVID-19 pneumonia. This lady had a history of multiple drug and alcohol use and medical non-compliance. She had been feeling ill for almost 2 weeks before she presented to our emergency department. Upon presentation she was quite short of breath, had low oxygen levels and her x-ray revealed extensive pneumonia in both lungs. A decision to admit her to the COVID-19 unit followed. She had been reluctant to accept being admitted to the hospital, as she had "several things pending". A review of her urine drug test revealed that she had recently abused marijuana, opioids, and cocaine.

On the first day of her hospitalizations, she requested to have large amount of narcotic as her *"whole body was in pain"*. When I asked her to be more specific, she told me that every part of her body was quite painful and she needed to use something like *"Dilaudid"*, which is a very potent (brand-name) narcotic analgesic. While opioids can be effective at treating pain when used as prescribed, they can also be highly addictive, and I am very careful as to how I prescribe them. When taken in larger doses or for longer periods than prescribed, opioids can lead to physical dependence, tolerance, and addiction. Opioid addiction is a chronic and relapsing condition that can have serious consequences, including overdose and death. When my patients request these agents without any specific reason, I find it difficult to provide such medications. So, I had a long conversation with the patient. I explained to her that she had been admitted to the hospital as she truly was quite ill and required in-hospital treatment and, that I wanted her to feel comfortable, but I could not offer her potent narcotics if I didn't have a precise reason for it. She was not happy, but accepted that she had a potentially life-threatening illness, and she needed treatment. Throughout the first night of hospitalization, she continued to request from the nurses the administration of narcotics for this "generalized pain" that she could not pinpoint.

The next morning when I was doing rounds, this lady was very agitated. I was concerned that she was withdrawing from some of her multiple drugs of abuse. She was being verbally abusive to the staff and was refusing a good number of her medications and treatments. I, again, explained to her the importance of compliance. This time, the main question was *"when could she leave the hospital?"*. When I told her, it probably would take between 4-7 days, she then asked, *"can I have a day pass, so I can take care of things at home?"*. In my experience, when these questions occur, it usually means that the patient is having cravings for some of the drugs of abuse. I requested that my team reach out to her family, to see if there was any issue that truly require immediate attention. The family indicated that *"everything was under control"*.

That night I got a call from the nurses at 3 am. Apparently, they found the patient running on the hallway and reaching one of the lateral exits of the COVID-19 unit. The nurses that were inside the COVID-19 unit, in full PPE were able to run after her and get her back to her room and hooked to the monitoring systems. The patient had told them that *"she was tired and wanted to go outside to smoke a cigarette"*. As the reader may know In COVID-19 units, cigarette smoking poses additional risks both for the smoker and those around them. Firstly, smoking in COVID-19 units can increase the risk of virus transmission. Smoking produces droplets and aerosols that can contain the virus and be spread to others. This puts healthcare workers, other patients, and visitors at risk of infection. Secondly, smoking can exacerbate the symptoms of COVID-19. COVID-19 primarily affects the respiratory system, and smoking can cause further damage to the lungs. This can make it more difficult for individuals to breathe and can worsen other symptoms, such as coughing. For these reasons, all COVID-19 units prohibit smoking on their premises. Patients who smoke are usually provided with nicotine replacement therapy, such as nicotine patches or gum, to help manage nicotine withdrawal symptoms. This was offered to the patient, but she refused. The next morning, we had another discussion about compliance, and risk to self and others, while she was being so ill. I told her to remember that escaping from a COVID-19 unit could have serious consequences. Patients who leave against medical advice risk worsening their condition or developing complications that require emergency medical attention. Furthermore, they may spread the virus to others, putting themselves and their loved ones at risk. She appeared to be listening to what I said, but I was not sure she understood.

Throughout the day, I came to see the patient multiple time to assure her that soon she would be able to be released, and that the best way to expedite the process, was by being complaint with the treatment. That same night, as soon as I left the hospital, I was called back in, as the nurses had seen the patient in the hallway cameras exiting the hospital. I was back at the hospital, and now, we had a missing patient.

Hospitals typically have protocols in place for handling patients who attempt to leave against medical advice or who escape. These protocols may involve contacting security personnel or law enforcement agencies to help locate the patient and ensure their safety. Staff may also communicate with the patient's family members or caregivers to inform them of the situation and enlist their help in finding the patient. We did all of these and still were unable to find her. I dispatched the security personnel to her home, but she had not gone there either.

Two days later, we got a call from another hospital, where the patient had been admitted with respiratory failure due to progression of her COVID-19 pneumonia and a cocaine overdose. The patient remained in such institution for several weeks, and eventually was discharged to home.

The Man Who Did Not Believe in COVID-19

During the COVID-19 pandemic there were many people that did not believe that the illness was real. Despite the overwhelming scientific evidence and public health recommendations, there were people who did not believe in the existence of COVID-19 or the severity of the disease. One reason why some people did not believe in COVID-19 was because of the misinformation that had been circulating on social media and other online platforms. The internet made it easier than ever for people to share information and opinions, but it also created an environment where false or misleading information could spread quickly. Some individuals used social media platforms to promote conspiracy theories about the origins of the virus, suggesting that it was part of a larger plot to control the population. Others downplayed the severity of the disease, claiming that it was no worse than the flu or that it only affected certain groups of people.

Another reason why some people did not believe in COVID-19 was because of the politicization of the pandemic. In many countries, political leaders took different approaches to the pandemic, with some downplaying the severity of the disease and others implementing strict lockdown measures. This led to a divide between people who supported one political party or leader versus those who supported another. As a result, some individuals rejected the advice of public health officials and scientists because it conflicted with their political beliefs.

As I saw this conflict, I always tried to approach patients in a very non-political manner, always respecting their beliefs. This was the case, up until the time, one of our staff members got sick.

As the COVID-19 pandemic was in full effect, our hospital was totally overwhelmed with patients who were dying. Every hospital in the Houston metropolitan area was having such a problem. At that point, the federal government decided to help one hospital in Houston, ours, by sending the military to assist us with additional nurses and, physicians. I remember the day I heard the news, I was so excited, as we were going to finally get some help. We created a separate COVID-19 unit for the Military that had everything they needed to care for these critically ill patients. The hospital administration helped the Military in every way to make this a smooth transition.

The hospital decided that we need to place at the entrance of the Military ward a security guard. This gentleman was a 67-year-old man that from the first day of the pandemic refused to believe that COVID-19 was a real illness. I remember talking to him several times and ask him to please wear a mask, to which he stated, *"masks do not work"*. At the time, there was limited information as to the utility of masks, and the consensus was to use them in an attempt to decrease the chances of contagion.

As the Military unit was opening, I saw this man again not wearing a mask. I approached him and asked him why was the doing this, to which he replied *"this is just a show....the Government sent the Military individuals just as a show, but there is no pandemic, it is all a lie"*. Our conversation rapidly became a political discussion in which he indicated a variety of conspiracy theories. He continued to refuse to wear a mask, as *"he had his right to do so"*.

Approximately a month later, I go a phone call at 3 a.m. from our emergency department indicating that this man was having severe shortness of breath, had a low oxygen and had just tested positive for COVID-19, but that was refusing to be admitted to the hospital. I remember that night, as I had literally just arrived home from a very busy day, but now I had to return to the hospital to convince him to be admitted, otherwise he would die. I then drove back to the hospital and went straight to the emergency department.

Upon arrival, I saw our security guard gasping for air, screaming at the emergency department nurse. He was telling her that she was a liar and that he just had a regular pneumonia. As I entered his cubicle, I told him that I had seen his chest imaging and that I was concerned about a severe pneumonia. He calmed down, as we had a good working relation, and to some extent, he trusted me. I mentioned that I had seen the COVID-19 result, but that I was going to repeat it, and that I truly thought it was in his best interest to stay in the hospital. To my surprise, he agreed to stay but requested to no where in his chart, we would add a diagnosis of COVID-19.

Once in the unit, he was started on our clinical management protocol for patients with severe COVID-19. He required supplemental oxygen by means of a high-flow nasal cannula initially. He continued to question his diagnosis to everyone that went into his room. I followed up on my promise to recheck his COVID-19 test and once I had it in my hands, I came back to see him. Once I handed him the result, he said *"this is a lie"*.

This was a very difficult situation, as I had a patient that did not believe in COVID-19, that had the disease and that was deadly ill. The patient kept on asking for "antibiotics" and not treatment for COVID-19. He was sure that it was all a big lie, and that he was being admitted to the hospital so that the hospital could justify its COVID-19 unit. The nurses were cursed at every single time they went to see him.

Within the next 48 hours, unfortunately, his condition rapidly deteriorated. He had developed clots in his lungs, even though he had received medications to prevent excessive coagulation. Coagulation is a natural process that occurs in the body to prevent excessive bleeding after an injury. However, in some COVID-19 patients, the virus can trigger an abnormal immune response that causes blood to clot excessively, leading to a range of complications. One of the most serious coagulation issues in COVID-19 patients was the formation of blood clots in the lungs, a condition known as pulmonary embolism. This occurs when a clot forms in the veins of the legs or arms and then travels to the lungs, where it can block blood flow and cause respiratory distress.

Our security guard required to be placed on assisted mechanical ventilation and his condition continued to deteriorate despite maximum medical efforts. His closest relatives were contacted, as it seemed that his prognosis was dismal. I met with his family and found out that the had denied the existence of the virus from the very beginning of the pandemic and had multiple conspiracy theories that he had shared with them. He had told me some of them, and yet, he was now on a ventilator fighting for his own life.

Despite every possible medical effort at saving his life, after 5 days of hospitalization, he succumbed. It is always tragic for a healthcare provider, when someone loses their life to a disease, especially when it could have been preventable. In this case of a patient who did not believe that COVID-19 was a real illness, and subsequently died from the disease, it is a stark reminder of the importance of why we had to take the pandemic seriously and follow public health guidelines. Misinformation and conspiracy theories lead to dangerous complacency in this man. In addition, puts individuals at higher risk of contracting the virus and experiencing severe symptoms.

The Sex Worker

I am sure you wonder what this chapter is all about, as prostitution is a practice that involves close physical contact and poses a high risk of transmitting COVID-19. During the pandemic, many countries where prostitution is legal, imposed strict measures to reduce the spread of the virus, including social distancing and restrictions on non-essential businesses. These measures significantly impacted the prostitution industry and raised concerns about the health and safety of sex workers. Yet, we had one unique patient that cared more about her customers, than her own health.

In late 2021, I admitted to our COVID-19 unit a 41-year-old lady with history of heavy tobacco and alcohol use, with severe cough, chills, low oxygen levels and a very abnormal chest radiograph. This lady was a sex worker in an area close to the hospital and had continued to work during the pandemic. On arrival to our unit, she was awake, alert, visibly having difficulty breathing, requiring the administration of oxygen via a nasal device. Her vital signs suggested that she could decompensate at any point. She was hooked to the monitor systems, received her first doses of the medications that we were using to treat such illness, and she was allowed to rest. I came to talk to her to find out that she had 11 children ranging from 2 to 25 years of age. I explained to her the process that she would undergo and how the COVID-19 unit worked, including the strict visitor policy that we were enforcing. She agreed to undergo treatment and follow our advice.

After three days in the hospital, this lady was improving significantly. Her oxygen requirements were now minimal, and I was anticipating discharging her home in the next couple of days. I was able to get to know more about her profession, and the fact that none of his children had ever met their fathers. She was quite aware about the other potential issues that she could have as a sex worker. Indeed, she had been treated multiple times for a variety of sexually transmitted disorders.

That same night, the patient saw another patient on the hallways that "appeared to be familiar" and decided to follow this individual to his room. The other patient was a 53-year-old homeless man that had been admitted with COVID-19 pneumonia and had not been able to be discharged, as he had no safe place to go to. This was the time, where even half-way houses would not accept new "tenants" due to the pandemic.

As the sex worker approached the room of this other patient, she confirmed that she knew who this man was and confronted him. According to the nursing staff, she started screaming at him that he had fathered one of her multiple children. The events escalated to the point that the security guards had to come to the COVID-19 unit to remove her and place her back in her room.

Sex work is a complex and multifaceted issue, that involves a wide range of social, economic, and cultural factors. One aspect of this issue is the potential for sex workers to become pregnant from their clients and later see those clients in their lives. This is exactly what happened to our patient. This situation can be challenging and emotionally charged for both parties involved. For the sex worker, it may bring up feelings of anger, resentment, or regret towards the "client", especially if the client was not supportive or understanding during the pregnancy or childbirth. Our patient was truly upset with this man, as apparently, he was aware of her pregnancy in the past.

On my morning rounds I spoke to the patient and listened to her story. I asked our social worker to try to intervene and obtain more information. The patient remained quite angry to find out that this man was in the hospital, and she elected to leave the hospital against medical advice (AMA).

Although the decision to leave the hospital AMA is a personal choice, it is important to understand the potential implications of such a decision. First and foremost, leaving the hospital AMA can significantly impact a patient's health. COVID-19 can be a severe and life-threatening disease, and patients who leave the hospital prematurely may not receive the proper medical care needed to combat the illness. For example, some COVID-19 patients require supplemental oxygen or other forms of respiratory support, and leaving the hospital AMA means they may not receive these necessary treatments. Our patient had the potential to deteriorate. Furthermore, leaving the hospital AMA can also increase the risk of complications and long-term health problems. COVID-19 can cause long-term damage to the lungs, heart, and other vital organs, and patients who leave the hospital prematurely may not receive the necessary treatment to prevent or minimize these long-term effects. Additionally, leaving the hospital before completing the recommended course of treatment can increase the risk of reinfection, which can be more severe than the initial infection.

Another implication of leaving the hospital AMA is the potential risk to the community. COVID-19 is highly contagious and can easily spread from person to person. Patients who leave the hospital prematurely may be contagious and can spread the virus to others, putting their family, friends, and community at risk. This is especially concerning for those who are immunocompromised, elderly, or have underlying health conditions that put them at a higher risk of severe illness or death. Moreover, leaving the hospital AMA can impact the healthcare system as a whole. Hospitals are already overwhelmed with COVID-19 patients, and patients who leave prematurely may take up a hospital bed that could have been used for another patient who needs medical attention. This can put a strain on the healthcare system and limit the resources available to those who truly need them.

Massage My Back and I Will Give You 100 Dollars

During the summer of 2020, a 67-year-old woman was transferred to my clinical service from an outside hospital, where she had presented 3 days prior to admission to my COVID-19 unit with high fever, shortness of breath and, extremely low oxygen levels that required the use of an artificial respirator. The family was not comfortable with the care the patient was receiving at the other hospital and decided to have her transferred to my care. At that time, the mortality rates for COVID-19 that were in hospitals across the World were more than 40 percent, while under my care were less than 5 percent. I would get patients every single day in transfer, as many have heard about the variety of different treatment approaches that we had and the success rates.

On arrival to our COVID-19 unit, this lady was critically ill, on an induced medical coma, fully sedated, requiring the maximum amount of oxygen that can be given to a patient via a respirator. In addition, her kidney function was terrible, and it was likely that she would require to be placed on an artificial kidney (dialysis). Her prognosis was poor, yet we were going to try everything to save her. That was our primary goal. The family was quite pleased that we had a management plan and were hopeful for success.

The first 24 hours in our unit were intense. I had to try a variety of modifications to the respirator to keep oxygen levels that would be compatible with life. At some point in time, I elected to use the "prone position". This position is when a person lies face down, with their chest and stomach against the bed. It is believed to be helpful in COVID-19 patients because it can improve oxygenation and reduce the need for mechanical ventilation. When a person is in the prone position, gravity helps to open the small air sacs in the lungs called alveoli, allowing more air to reach them. This can improve the exchange of oxygen and carbon dioxide in the lungs, which can help increase oxygen levels in the body. Additionally, being in the prone position can help improve blood flow to the lungs, reducing the risk of blood clots that can be a complication of COVID-19. Very early in the pandemic we found that the prone position was a simple, non-invasive intervention that can potentially improve outcomes in COVID-19 patients by improving oxygenation and reducing the need for more invasive treatments. In our patient's case, the prone position clearly helped and within a period of just hours, her oxygen levels were much better, and we were able to slowly start weaning her from the artificial respirator.

The next morning, her oxygen levels were good enough that we placed her on her back, and I made a request to decrease the amount of sedation to assess her mental state. The level of sedation in the critically ill patients is usually assessed using a combination of objective measurements and subjective observations. Among the objective measurements, we include things like monitoring the patient's vital signs (such as heart rate, blood pressure, and oxygen saturation), using specialized equipment to measure brain activity, and administering standardized sedation scales (such as the Richmond Agitation-Sedation Scale or the Sedation-Agitation Scale). These scales rate a patient's level of sedation on a numerical scale, typically ranging from -5 (unresponsive) to +4 (very agitated). On the other hand, subjective observations may include assessing the patient's responsiveness to verbal or physical stimuli, monitoring their level of agitation or restlessness, and evaluating their ability to follow simple commands or communicate with caregivers.

Late that afternoon, the patient appeared awake but was somewhat agitated, trying to point towards her wrists. Many of our patients, while sedated, required to be restrained to prevent them from pulling the monitoring equipment and more importantly, allow disconnection from the respirator. While I was visiting her, and seeing her reaction, I explained to her what was going on, and the importance of avoiding disconnection from the respirator. I also told her she was unable to talk, as she had a tube that went through her vocal cords, but if she needed to write something, I could arrange for a writing board, so we could communicate. She understood and requested the writing board. Writing boards, also known as communication boards, are commonly used in ICUs to facilitate communication between healthcare providers and patients who are unable to speak or have difficulty communicating verbally. These boards can be particularly useful for patients who are on respirators (mechanical ventilation) or have other conditions that limit their ability to communicate. Writing boards typically consist of a whiteboard or tablet with various pre-printed or customizable sections, that allow patients to convey their needs and preferences. These sections may include things such as basic information about the patient (such as their name and date of birth), common medical procedures or treatments (such as suctioning or medication administration), pain or discomfort levels, requests for water, food, or other basic needs, yes/no or multiple-choice questions to help clarify patient preferences or concerns. In addition to these pre-printed sections, writing boards may also have space for patients or caregivers to write or draw additional information as needed. Some boards may also include pictures or symbols to help patients who have difficulty reading or writing.

As soon as our patient got her communication board, she wrote with a tremulous hand *"massage my back and I will give you 100 dollars"*. The nurse came out of her room into the nurses' station to find me and told me what she had written. As this was early in the pandemic, all the equipment used in the rooms of patients with COVID-19 had to stay there and could not be moved into "clean areas". As I was told this unique request from the patient, I decided to go back into her room and inquire if she had pain or some other discomfort for which she was requesting a massage.

As I entered her room, I saw the communication board and clearly identified the words she had written. Indeed, she was asking the healthcare providers for a back massage and in exchange she was offering 100 dollars. I asked her about this unique request and, using the same communication board, indicated that her back muscles had been cramping for days prior to admission. She also indicated using the communication board, that she had regular massages for chronic back issues. At that point, I proceeded to find out where the discomfort was and gently massaged the area. I also told her she did not have to pay me the 100 dollars!

Within 48 hours I was able to wean her from the respirator, and once she was able to talk, she expressed her gratitude for the massage. I made sure that our staff would provide her with brief periods of massage, up until the time of discharge. The patient did quite well, despite our initial concerns for a guarded prognosis, and to date, she follows in my office on regular basis. She continues to get regular back massages.

Massage therapy was beneficial in managing some of the symptoms associated with COVID-19, such as stress, anxiety, and muscle tension. Massage therapy can help alleviate stress and anxiety by promoting relaxation and reducing muscle tension. It can also improve circulation and promote lymphatic drainage, which can help the body's immune system function more efficiently. Our patient was quite pleased to receive this therapeutic intervention.

The Man That Had Fun by Himself

There is always that one patient that you will never be able to forget. Such was the case of this 32-year-old married gentleman that was admitted very early in the pandemic to our COVID-19 unit in critical condition after suffering with this illness for approximately 10 days. As this man was an illegal immigrant, he was very concerned about coming to the hospital and waited until he was almost unable to breath before he presented to our emergency department. On arrival to the hospital, he was quite short of breath, with oxygen levels that were very low, suffering from high fevers and was clearly very dehydrated.

Once he entered the COVID-19 unit, he was immediately placed on an assisted supplemental oxygen delivery system using a bilevel positive pressure ventilator called BiPAP. This device works by providing two different levels of air pressure: one higher pressure level during inhalation (when the patient is breathing in), and a lower pressure level during exhalation (when the patient is breathing out). This helps to keep the airways open and prevent the collapse of the lung tissue, which can be particularly helpful for people with conditions such as sleep apnea, chronic obstructive pulmonary disease (COPD), or acute respiratory failure, such as the case of our patient. The BiPAP machine is composed of a small device that is connected to a mask worn over the patient's nose and/or mouth. The machine delivers air to the patient through the mask, which is secured in place with straps. Many of our patients find this uncomfortable, but it is much better than the alternative, which it to be placed on a respirator with a tube in the trachea (wind pipe).

This man's lungs were damaged significantly, and such illness was not only causing problems with the lungs, but also with the heart. An ultrasound revealed that the pressure of the area of his heart connected to the lungs was extremely high. At that point, we had to look for ways to decrease such pressure levels with medications. There are several medications that can help decrease the pressure in such vessels (pulmonary hypertension), by relaxing the blood vessels in the lungs and improving blood flow. These may include some called calcium channel blockers, prostacyclin analogs, endothelin receptor antagonists, and phosphodiesterase type 5 (PDE5) inhibitors. The latter is widely used for other conditions such as erectile dysfunction. Indeed, sildenafil (Viagra™) was originally developed to treat patients with high pressures in their pulmonary arteries. The common side effect that was seen in those using it, penis erection, made it a medication of choice for those suffering with issues related to erectile dysfunction. Yet, as we were fighting an illness where we have limited options, many clinicians were using Sildenafil in patients as sick as this man in hopes to decrease that abnormal pressure in the vessels connecting the heart and the lungs and improving oxygenation.

Our patient was started on low doses of sildenafil and was carefully monitored. His oxygenation improved after 24 hours. I was unsure if this was related to our cocktail of medications or the addition of this agent to his treatment. Like many patients in the COVID-19 unit, we would give them several medications at the same time hoping for the best. Remember, this was a war against an invisible enemy that was killing people by the thousands every single day. As the patient oxygen levels had improved, we decided to slowly decrease his BiPAP support and eventually we were able to have him on a nasal cannula connected to his nose. At this point, we provided him with a cellular phone so he could videoconference with his spouse a few times a day.

On the 6th hospital day, I was called by one of the nurses that had "caught" the patient masturbating while video calling his spouse. The patient apparently had also been found to do the same the prior night by another nurse. Every time, the patient had stated that "out of the blue he had an erection" and immediately had called his spouse. When I was told this, I went in to speak to him and explained in great detail that the most likely reason of these "unexplained erections" was the fact that we were using Sildenafil on him. He stated that he was "ashamed" and I reassured him that there was nothing to be ashamed off, as this was an expected side effect of the medication, and he seemed to have a good relationship with his spouse.

Over the next few days, I was able to slowly wean the sildenafil and his oxygen. After a few days the patient was discharged to his home in stable condition. He was seen on the outpatient COVID-19 clinic a couple of weeks later where he was found to be much better.

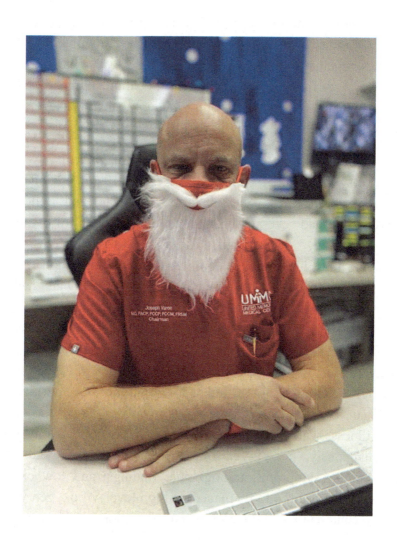

The Conjugal Visit

As mentioned in prior cases, it was relatively common to admit 2 or more members of the same family to our COVID-19 unit, as many times they were all exposed to the same individual that got them this illness. In our unit, we attempted to keep couples together, wherever it was possible. On some occasions this was a difficult task due to bed allocation, number of male versus female patients and other factors (such as severity of illness, need for several life-sustaining devices at bedside).

In the winter of 2020, we received 2 patients from the emergency department with severe COVID-19 pneumonia. One was a 51-year-old man with a history of diabetes and high blood pressure that had several days of fever and shortness of breath. In the emergency department, his x-rays showed pneumonia involving both lungs and a significant drop in his blood oxygen levels. Of note, this man did not believe in COVID-19 and had not followed any of the recommendations regarding social distancing or masking. Even as he was getting admitted, he stated that he did not have COVID-19, despite a positive test and that we were trying to get him admitted just to increase the revenue of the hospital. After a few hours, and as his condition was deteriorating, he began to understand that he was critically ill likely due to this viral illness, which he had denied existed for quite a long time. Simultaneously, his 39-year-old girlfriend was being admitted with similar symptoms, radiographic findings, and low oxygen levels. Both required to be placed on high levels of oxygen with a special cannula that delivered high concentrations of this gas.

As we did not have an empty room where we could accommodate both patients, we had to place the lady with another COVID-19 woman in a double room, and close by we admitted the man to a room where there was a man on a mechanical respirator in a coma. The lady was quite upset that she was not being admitted to the same room as her boyfriend. On those days, our COVID-19 was completely full, and we had up to 88 in patients at any given time. You can imagine the amount of work that caring for all those patients at the same time had. Our team was outstanding at dealing with multiple issues at the same time, yet it was impossible to "please" every request for accommodations.

Both patients were treated with our cocktail of medications, supplemental oxygen, and excellent nursing care. Over the first 48 hours, their improvement in symptoms was quite significant and I was quite sure that their outcome would be reasonable, and they probably could be released in a short period time. However, both patients were requesting to be moved together to the same room. Unfortunately, the bed allocation was full, and this was not a consideration that we could accomplish.

That night, I was called by the nursing staff at 330 a.m. to inform me that the lady had gone into her boyfriend's room. When I asked the nurse to please go into the room and take her to her room, she indicated that *"they went to ask her to leave the room, but when they entered the room, they found her having sex with the boyfriend"*. I must admit that I have seen this way too many times in my professional career and reminded me of a conjugal visit. These kinds of visits, however, are usually scheduled between an inmate in prison and their spouse or intimate partner, during which they are allowed to spend time together in a private setting, typically for a few hours or overnight. These visits are also sometimes called "family visits" or "extended visits." Even though I believe that these visits may be therapeutic to some extent as the purpose of conjugal visits is to maintain family ties and relationships, and to provide a means for inmates to have physical contact with their loved ones, in our context of critically ill patients, are not recommended. The patients were having sex in a bed next to a patient that was on a coma on an artificial respirator.

The next morning, I saw both patients and discussed with them how dangerous had been their intimate time the prior night. Both decided that they wanted to leave the hospital against medical advice. We never heard about them again.

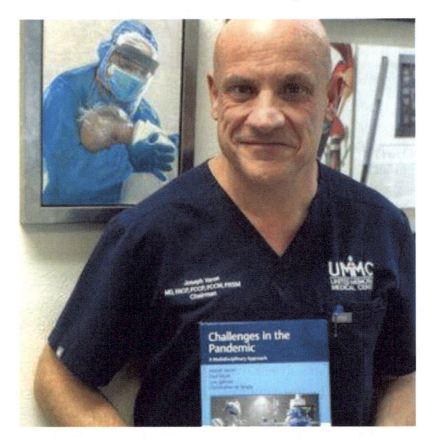

The Screamer

In the COVID-19 unit we frequently had chaotic days, where critically ill patients were having significant issues, new patients were coming in and a plethora of complaints were noted. However, one that was particularly difficult to address was a patient that would start screaming. Remember, in COVID-19 units, patients experienced a range of symptoms, from mild to severe, including difficulty breathing, fever, cough, and fatigue. In most cases, patients required oxygen therapy, some form of help with respiration, or other forms of respiratory support to manage their symptoms. Unfortunately, in some instances, patients inside COVID-19 units screamed or vocalized their distress. This was quite a distressing experience for both patients and healthcare providers.

In late May 2021, we admitted a 94-year-old woman with a history of lung cancer, who was undergoing chemotherapy, to our unit with fever, chills, protracted cough, and clinical evidence of severe COVID-19 pneumonia. Our initial concern was the fact that this lady had a lung cancer and on top of that, she had COVID-19, therefore her prognosis was guarded. She had no close family members and used to live alone with her dog in an apartment close to the hospital.

Despite the potential lethal outcome in this lady, we provided her with state-of-the-art medical care in our unit. On arrival to our unit, she was awake, alert, and conversational and was able to tell us her onset of symptoms. I explained to her in detail what our COVID-19 protocol consisted of, and she agreed to receive medical treatment. I was quite impressed with how sharp this lady was. She was hooked to the monitors, supplemental oxygen, and started to receive treatment. She really looked like a "poster child" for a compliant patient with treatment.

Less than 24 hours after her admission, I was called to her bedside as she had removed all her monitoring devices, had stood up from her bed and walked to the hallway and started to scream *"they are trying to kill me"*. I could hear her screams from the nurses' station, despite the containment barriers we had. These containment barriers were an essential part of COVID-19 units in hospitals and healthcare facilities. These barriers were designed to prevent the spread of the virus between patients and healthcare workers, and to ensure that the unit remained a safe environment for everyone involved.

As I entered the COVID-19 unit, I saw our patient walking towards the exit, with blood dripping from her arm, as she had pulled an intravenous line she had, and screaming profoundly that she *"needed to go home to take care of her dog"*. I got close to her and held her hand and asked her to come with me to her room, so we could chat. Yet, she kept on screaming. I did not know if this was the effect of one of the medications, if she was having a stroke, or if these were the ill effects of low oxygen on her body. However, I had to do something to get her to relax, so I could figure out what was going on. This was a fragile, old lady that could get in trouble anytime. I remembered, that in many instances, patients inside COVID-19 units had to be "talked down" as those who were experiencing severe symptoms felt frightened, confused, or disoriented, and struggled to communicate effectively with their caregivers. Many of our patients were frustrated, in fear, and in many instances even panic. For healthcare providers working in COVID-19 units, dealing with patients who were screaming or vocalizing their distress was really challenging. These providers were often working long hours under stressful conditions and were also dealing with their own fears and concerns related to the virus.

My patient agreed to walk back to her room. I was asking her more information about her dog. As I am a "dog lover", I told her about all the dogs I have, and she calmed down to some extent.

Once in her room, I could tell she was really frightened. This was interesting, as she was not scared about her lung cancer, but she was truly afraid of dying from COVID-19. Under normal circumstances, in order to help manage the emotional and psychological impact of hospitalization on patients, many facilities have a range of support measures. These may include counseling services, meditation or mindfulness programs, and other stress-reducing activities. However, during COVID-19, it was almost impossible to get any of them, as those individuals providing those services would not enter a COVID-19 unit.

After almost an hour of talking to the patient, I was able to get her to stop screaming and I promised her that I would send someone to her home to check on her pet. She calmed down significantly. I also wanted to know why she thought *"we were trying to kill her"*. She told me that because she was old, she thought we didn't want her to survive. I explained to her, that the fact that she was 94 and still alive and fighting lung cancer was remarkable and that I would fight to keep her alive, no matter what. She smiled!

One of the members of my team went to her home and found her dog. The pet was in good health. My team member decided to keep the dog in her home while the patient was still in the hospital. Our patient was grateful that we were caring for her beloved pet. She complied with the rest of her medical treatment.

It took close to a week, before I was comfortable to say that this lady had survived severe COVID-19 in the context of lung cancer at the age of 94. I was so happy that she had done so well that I made her a trophy that said, *"I beat COVID-19"* and gave it to her as she was leaving the hospital. I made sure she had all the help she needed at home. Her dog came back to her home after she had been there for a few days. To date, I continue to follow her in my outpatient clinic. Her lung cancer is controlled, and she is still mentally intact and has never screamed at me again.

The Birthday Party

Throughout the COVID-19 pandemic, our unit remained extremely busy. Despite such adversity, I always made it a priority to have *"fun"* in our unit. Coping with the stress and anxiety of working or being treated in a COVID-19 unit was challenging and finding ways to have fun and relax were an effective coping mechanism. However, we had to prioritize the safety of everyone involved and follow all COVID-19 protocols and guidelines. For example, during Halloween, I asked all the personnel to decorate their PPE so that they would make our patients smile when they went into their confined rooms.

On January of 2021, we admitted to our COVID-19 unit a 34-year-old gentleman who had recently moved to the United States from Cuba with his family. This man spoke no English, was married, and had two children. He had no significant medical conditions and had developed symptoms for 2 weeks prior to admission, but as he had no medical insurance and had issues with his legal status on the country, had refused to come to the hospital for medical care. On the day of admission, he was having fever, chills, severe cough, and was extremely short of breath. In the emergency department, imaging of his lungs revealed severe pneumonia. His oxygen levels were so low that he had to be started on non-invasive respiratory support utilizing a BiPAP device. In COVID-19 patients, we found early in the pandemic, BiPAP could be used to manage respiratory distress and prevent the need for intubation (placing a tube in the windpipe) and mechanical ventilation. However, BiPAP was not well tolerated in all patients. For example, the masks used for BiPAP therapy were uncomfortable for some patients, causing irritation, pressure points, and other discomforts. The air pressure delivered by the BiPAP machine was also uncomfortable for some patients, causing feelings of bloating, pressure, or difficulty exhaling. The noise generated by the BiPAP machine was disruptive in some patients and prevented them from getting a good night's sleep. But the most important concern with the use of this device was that many patients felt claustrophobic wearing a mask over their face, making BiPAP therapy uncomfortable or intolerable. This was the case of our patient.

As soon as we started this therapeutic intervention, he immediately started screaming and telling us that we could not tolerate it (in Spanish). I explained to him in detail that the alternative was to place a tube in his throat and sedate him, but that more than 80% of patients that were placed on respirators with COVID-19 would die. It took a while to get him to relax, but eventually he was able to tolerate the device. I was very concerned, as I had seen many young individuals that had ended up on a respirator that had not survived this lethal illness.

The first 72 hours of his hospitalization were quite difficult. He had significant changes in oxygenation and was extremely anxious. However, we were fighting this war against the virus together and he was now being compliant. I was carefully optimistic that we would win. But like most patients who are critically ill, at the end of the third day, he started to worsen again. This time, his blood pressure started to fall, and I was concerned he was developing a secondary infection. Secondary infections occurred in individuals with COVID-19, just like with any other viral infection. COVID-19 weakens the immune system, making it easier for other opportunistic infections to occur. Secondary infections can be bacterial or fungal and are often caused by organisms that are normally present in the body. In this man's case, he was developing a fungal infection that we started to treat right away.

As the fungal infection was being treated, the patient started to be extremely depressed. I did not know at the time, if this was part of the illness, the medications or some underlying psychiatric condition. As soon as it was safe to allow him to be of the BiPAP device for a few minutes, I sat with him and asked him what was going on and why was he so sad. He told me *"my daughter turns 2 years of age tomorrow and I will not be with her"*. That was the turning point for me, I had to do something to make this man smile again. At that point I planned a virtual birthday party for his child.

Preparing for a virtual birthday party can be a fun and creative way to celebrate with friends and family, while still maintaining social distancing. I had never prepared one in my life. I called the patient's spouse, and I told her my team and I were going to prepare a party for her daughter. As this family had limited resources, she was very appreciative to hear such news. My team found a great bakery that made 2 "Minnie Mouse" cakes. One would be delivered to the patient's home and the other one to the hospital. We sent to his house a variety of decorations, so that the spouse could create a festive atmosphere. The next morning, in the patient's room, we put up balloons, streamers, and even a birthday banner. We coordinated with all the members of our team to make sure everyone has their favorite food or snack to enjoy during the party. We were going to have a party in the middle of chaos.

The next step was to assure we had presents for the patient's daughter and that they would be delivered on time to the party. My team got the child a variety of age-appropriate presents that were delivered the morning of the party. We had not told my patient as to the party, and we had asked the spouse not to share such information when we did videoconferencing with her, so she could see her husband the night prior to the event.

On the day of the party, I got my team to go into the patient room, in full PPE as always, to decorate his room. He was puzzled as to what was going on, as we were placing balloons and many other decorations. I told him we were going to have a birthday party for his daughter, and he smiled. I also told him I would get him off the BiPAP for a few minutes during the party, so he could taste the birthday cake we had gotten for him (an identical one was sent to his daughter). This man was ill but now I could see a smile in his face. That afternoon we had a party. I had asked several members of the team to come into the room to sing happy birthday to his daughter via video conference. You could see on the screen the child eating cake and opening her presents. The patient was very happy.

Over the next couple of weeks, this man remained in the hospital but slowly improved. He still was requiring oxygen, but he was alive. I was able to discharge him to home after a stormy hospital course on home oxygen. He followed up in our clinic a few weeks later and was extremely appreciative of the virtual party we had for his daughter.

This was a very gratifying experience to my team and I. COVID-19 had a significant impact on mental health, with many patients experiencing anxiety, depression, and other emotional issues. When the healthcare team can help patients cope with these challenges, it can be very rewarding.

About the Author

Dr. Varon is a Professor at the University of Houston College of Medicine. He is the Chairman and President of Dorrington Medical Associates. Formerly, he served as Chairman of the Board of United Memorial Medical Center Premier and United General Hospital. He is Chief of Critical Care and COVID-19 unit at United Memorial Medical Center. Dr. Varon is the Former Chief of Critical Care Services and Past Chief of Staff at United Memorial Medical Center and University General Hospital. He is a Professor of Medicine, Surgery and Professor of Emergency Medicine at several universities in Mexico, the Middle East and Europe. He is the Associate Dean for the Caribbean Medical University.

After completing medical training at the UNAM Medical School in Mexico City, Mexico, Dr. Varon served as internship in internal medicine at Providence Hospital/George Washington University, Washington, D.C. A subsequent residency in internal medicine was completed at Stanford University School of Medicine in Stanford, California. Dr. Varon also served fellowships in critical care medicine and pulmonary diseases at Baylor College of Medicine in Houston. An avid researcher, Dr, Varon has contributed more than 850 peer-reviewed journal articles, 12 full textbooks, and 15 dozen book chapters to the medical literature. He is also a reviewer for multiple journals and currently serves as Editor-in-Chief for *Critical Care and Shock* and *Current Respiratory Medicine Reviews*.

Dr. Varon has won many prestigious awards and is considered among one of the top physicians in the United States. Dr. Varon is also known for his groundbreaking contributions to Critical Care Medicine in the fields of cardiopulmonary resuscitation and therapeutic hypothermia. He has developed and studied technology for selective brain cooling. He is also a well-known expert in the area of hypertensive crises management. With Dr. Carlos Ayus, he co-described the hyponatremia associated to extreme exercise syndrome also known as the "Varon-Ayus syndrome" and with Mr. James Boston co-described the healthcare provider anxiety syndrome also known as the "Boston-Varon syndrome". Dr. Varon has lectured in over 60 different countries around the globe. Along with Professor Luc Montagnier (Nobel Prize Winner for Medicine in 2008), Dr. Varon created the Medical Prevention and Research Institute in Houston, Texas, where they conduct work on basic sciences projects.

Dr. Varon has appeared in over 3000 National and International television and radio shows with his techniques and care of patients. Dr. Varon is well known for his academic and clinical work in the management of acute hypertension and has published extensively on this subject. In addition, Dr. Varon has worked on studies related to ethical issues in acute care medicine and has several peer-reviewed publications on this controversial subject. In the past 38 months, Dr. Varon has become a world leader for his work on COVID-19 and his co-development of the MATH+ protocol to care for these patients. For this, he has received multiple awards, including a proclamation by the Mayor of the City of Houston of the "Dr. Joseph Varon Day". Dr. Varon also won the "Houston Humanitarian Award" for his work during the COVID-19 pandemic. In 2021, Dr. Varon was presented the "Global Citizen Award" by the United Nations.

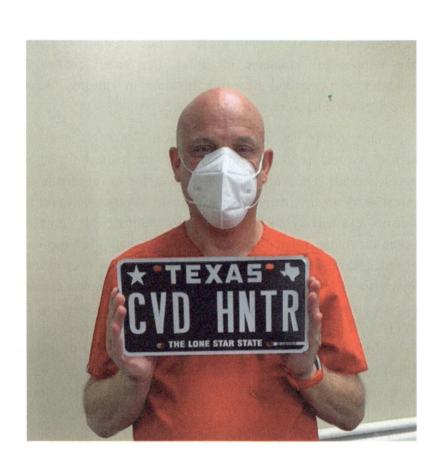

Made in the USA
Coppell, TX
12 July 2023

19076884R00075